The 24-Hour Horror Story with ChatGPT

Andrew Parry

Published by Andrew Parry, 2025.

THE 24-HOUR HORROR STORY WITH CHATGPT

First edition. April 11, 2025.

ISBN: 979-8230356011

Written by Andrew Parry.

Table of Contents

Why You Can Write a Horror Story in One Day

Let me tell you a little secret right from the start. You don't need weeks or months locked away in a candlelit room, pulling your hair out to write a spine-chilling horror story. You can actually write a fully structured, terrifying, and gripping horror narrative in a single day. Sounds like madness, right? It's not. In fact, once you learn how to use the tools in front of you—especially ChatGPT—you'll realize how ridiculously achievable it is.

The myth that writing a story, especially a horror story, has to be a long, torturous process is one of the biggest reasons so many people never start or never finish. They think it's about bleeding on the page, day after day, draft after draft, as if every writer has to suffer. That's nonsense. If you want to suffer, you can read your first draft out loud to your friends at midnight in a dark basement. That's scary. But writing it? That's supposed to be fun, fast, and a little bit dangerous.

The real reason you can write a horror story in a single day is because of three things: structure, mindset, and the power of modern AI like ChatGPT. Once you understand how to lean on those three pillars, writing becomes a process of assembling pieces rather than wandering through a foggy haunted forest hoping to find the plot.

First, let's talk about structure. Horror stories may feel chaotic, terrifying, and unpredictable when you're reading or watching them, but underneath, they're actually built on solid, predictable bones. Every great horror tale has a setup, rising tension, a middle where everything goes wrong, and an ending that leaves your heart pounding—or your skin crawling. That structure never changes. The haunted house has rooms, the forest has trees, the monster has sharp teeth. Once you know how to frame that structure, you can literally plug in characters, situations, twists, and scares like putting puzzle pieces together.

And guess what? You don't even have to start at the beginning. In this book, I'm going to teach you to start at the end. That's right. Start with the moment when the axe falls, the ghost whispers their final warning, the protagonist takes their last breath, or the monster's true identity is revealed. When you start with the ending in mind, you know exactly where you're heading. That's how professionals do it, and it cuts hours and hours of creative guesswork out of the process.

The second thing you need to believe is that writing a story doesn't have to be perfect in the first draft. One of the biggest lies writers tell themselves is that they have to get everything just right before they can move on. Forget that. When you write a horror story in one day, you're writing fast, raw, and unapologetically messy. You're putting down bones and blood. You can fix the spelling and finesse the metaphors later. Right now, the goal is to get the story out of your head and onto the page before it eats you alive.

That brings me to the third point—why today, more than ever before, you can actually pull this off. You have ChatGPT at your fingertips. That means you've got a creative assistant, research buddy, brainstorming partner, and writing machine all rolled into one. When you're stuck, ChatGPT unsticks you. When you're unsure how to describe the look of the monster creeping up the stairs, ChatGPT can give you five terrifying options in thirty seconds. When you need a name for the cursed town your story takes place in, you don't have to waste time flipping through baby name websites—you just ask.

This tool isn't here to write the story for you; it's here to work alongside you, to help you move faster without sacrificing creativity. It's like having a horror geek best friend who never sleeps, doesn't need coffee breaks, and is always ready to bounce ideas around. Together, you can generate characters, dialogue, scares, twists, and even the entire plot skeleton in a matter of minutes. That's how people are cranking out entire horror novels in weeks—but I'm here to show you how to crank out a solid, scary short story or novella in a single day.

The most important thing you need to do is shift your mindset. If you sit down to write thinking, "This is going to take forever," guess what? It will. But if you sit down with the attitude that you're about to build something fun, thrilling, and messy—and that you have the tools to do it—you'll move like lightning. Horror is built on momentum, and so is writing. When you're rolling, ideas stack on top of each other like bodies in a slasher flick. And when you're writing fast, you bypass the inner critic who wants to slow you down and make you second guess every sentence.

Think of writing your horror story like a one-day challenge. It's like setting out to build a haunted house in your backyard before the sun goes down. You don't have time to overthink whether the blood looks real enough. You've got to get the walls up, the doors creaking, and the shadows moving because trick-or-treaters are already on their way.

This approach also taps into the natural energy of fear itself. Fear is immediate. Fear is fast. Fear is a primal reaction. The longer you stew over every sentence, the more you distance yourself from the raw energy that makes horror stories work. But when you write in one day, you're riding the wave of that adrenaline. You're writing in the same pulse as your readers will read. That's how you write horror that actually scares people.

And here's something else nobody tells you: you already know how to scare people. You've been scared. You know what freaks you out in movies, in books, in dark alleys at night. All you have to do is bring that feeling to the page and use ChatGPT to help you shape it into a story. You don't have to invent fear—you just have to bottle it and pour it into a narrative.

So why can you write a horror story in one day? Because the structure is simple, the mindset is everything, and the tools are right here in front of you. Because horror is the most fun you can have while making people uncomfortable. Because you can ride the fear instead of dragging it behind you. And because perfection is the enemy of productivity.

By the end of this book, you'll have a full playbook, from idea to finished draft, showing you exactly how to pull this off. You'll know how to sketch out your premise, build the framework, develop terrifying characters, plant scary seeds in your plot, and tie it all up with a punchy, haunting ending—all in a single day. And you'll do it with ChatGPT helping you generate content, solve problems, and keep the creative engine roaring without ever running out of fuel.

So, if you've ever dreamed of writing a horror story but thought you didn't have the time, the patience, or the talent, I'm here to tell you: you do. All you need is one day, a little focus, and a willingness to scare the hell out of yourself while you're at it.

Tomorrow, we dive into how to unleash ChatGPT and get those terrifying ideas flowing. But for now, just know that writing a horror story in one day isn't a gimmick. It's a superpower. And by the end of this book, it'll be yours.

How ChatGPT Becomes Your Horror Co-Writer

Let's get one thing clear from the start—you're not writing this horror story alone. You've got a partner, a creative ally, a digital co-writer who doesn't sleep, doesn't complain, doesn't get writer's block, and never runs out of terrifying ideas. That partner is ChatGPT. And if you know how to work with it the right way, it's like having Stephen King, Jordan Peele, and H.P. Lovecraft whispering story ideas in your ear while you type.

Most people don't understand how to properly use a tool like ChatGPT when it comes to writing fiction. They either expect it to do everything for them, or they don't trust it at all. But the real magic happens when you treat it like a creative partner, not a machine. When you drive the creative direction and let ChatGPT assist you, fill in gaps, spark new ideas, and help you stay productive, you'll be shocked at how fast and fun the process becomes.

Think of ChatGPT like a horror story generator that's waiting to follow your lead. It's not going to write the perfect story for you on its own—it's not supposed to. What it will do is help you generate dozens of options, spit out ideas you wouldn't have thought of, and do all the heavy lifting when it comes to structure, descriptions, dialogue, pacing, and even the scary stuff.

Here's how this partnership works in practice. You start by giving ChatGPT a clear, specific prompt. Not something vague like "Write a scary story," but something like, "Help me come up with five terrifying horror story ideas about a haunted underground train station." The clearer and more specific you are, the better ChatGPT performs. It doesn't create out of thin air; it follows your lead, so the more you feed it, the more it gives back.

Once you've got an idea, ChatGPT can help you flesh it out. You can ask it to outline the plot in three acts. You can ask it to describe your main character's deepest fear. You can ask it to give you ten creepy names for the abandoned town your story is set in. And because it doesn't get tired or distracted, you can keep throwing questions at it until you've built the entire skeleton of your story.

But that's not all. ChatGPT is also fantastic at filling in the gaps when you get stuck. Every writer hits a wall eventually, even when they're writing fast. You'll get halfway through a scene and wonder, "What would the killer say here?" or "How do I describe the feeling of the walls closing in without sounding cheesy?" Instead of wasting time staring at the screen, you can simply ask ChatGPT. It'll give you multiple options in seconds, and nine times out of ten, one of them will be exactly what you need—or it'll spark a better idea in your own head.

Another huge advantage of using ChatGPT as your horror co-writer is how it helps you overcome the perfection trap. Too many writers waste time trying to make every sentence shine on the first draft. But when you're working with ChatGPT, you can pump out raw material fast, knowing that you can clean it up later. You don't need to worry about perfect prose while you're building your horror world; you just need to get the blood flowing and the shadows moving. ChatGPT keeps the pace going so you don't lose momentum.

And let's talk about world-building, because horror stories live and die by their setting. Whether your story takes place in an abandoned asylum, a remote mountain cabin, or a cursed seaside town, ChatGPT can help you create the world quickly and vividly. You can ask it to list creepy landmarks, invent local folklore, or describe the weather on the night everything goes wrong. Within minutes, you'll have pages of material you can drop straight into your story—or rewrite in your own voice.

Then there's character creation. Horror stories work best when the audience connects to the characters and cares whether they live or die. With ChatGPT, you can instantly brainstorm unique character traits, backstories, fears, and flaws. You can even ask for quick character sketches like, "Give me a protagonist who's terrified of drowning and has a tragic past connected to water." And boom—you'll get a ready-made character blueprint to work from.

The best part? You control everything. ChatGPT won't take over your story. It's not going to overwrite your ideas or force you to follow a certain plotline. It's here to serve you, to throw ideas at the wall so you can pick what sticks. You're still the storyteller, the one in charge, the director of this nightmare. You use ChatGPT like a creative assistant who works at the speed of light.

Now, let's be honest about something else. Horror stories aren't just about monsters and mayhem—they're about atmosphere, dread, tension, and psychological fear. Sometimes, it's hard to describe that feeling in words without sounding cliché or over-the-top. That's where ChatGPT really shines. You can ask it to describe how a character feels when they realize they're being watched. Or how the air feels in a basement where something evil lives. You can even feed it a sentence and ask it to rewrite it in a more chilling, poetic, or violent tone.

This kind of collaborative writing isn't just efficient; it's exciting. You'll find yourself in a creative flow state where the ideas keep coming because you've got someone—or something—feeding you new angles, unexpected twists, and creepy visuals. It's like having a horror writing jam session, and every suggestion makes the story stronger.

You might be wondering, though, "Isn't it cheating?" No, it's not. Because the story still comes from you. You're making the choices, setting the tone, steering the plot. ChatGPT isn't writing the story for you; it's writing it with you. And frankly, who cares how you get there if the result is a horror story that grips readers by the throat?

One thing I always recommend when working with ChatGPT is to treat the first draft like raw clay. Get as much material as you can in one sitting—idea, outline, characters, scenes, descriptions, dialogue—and don't worry about how rough it is. You can spend another day later sculpting, polishing, editing. But your goal here is to create the entire story skeleton, flesh and blood, in one day. ChatGPT makes that not only possible but fun.

You're also going to learn how to instruct ChatGPT better as you go. The more you use it, the better you'll get at asking for exactly what you need. You'll develop a rhythm, a workflow where you're bouncing ideas back and forth at high speed. You'll start seeing the gaps before they appear and knowing how to plug them in minutes. It becomes a creative conversation—a creepy, thrilling, productive one.

So by now, you should already see how powerful this collaboration can be. ChatGPT isn't your enemy, and it's not a crutch. It's your horror writing partner, ready to help you generate ideas, structure your plot, build terrifying worlds, develop memorable characters, and keep you writing fast without ever losing steam.

In the next chapter, we're going to talk about how to start at the end. Why horror stories become more powerful when you work backward and how ChatGPT can help you reverse-engineer the scariest, bloodiest, most chilling ending and then build your entire story around it.

Because now that you've got your creative partner in place, it's time to start constructing your nightmare.

The Secret to Starting with the Ending

Here's where we start to really flip the script. Most people sit down to write a horror story and immediately try to come up with a beginning—a creepy opening scene, a dark and stormy night, maybe a victim running through the woods. But that's the slow way, the hard way, and honestly, it's why so many writers never finish. Because if you don't know where you're going, it's easy to get lost in the dark.

I'm here to tell you the real secret weapon to writing a gripping, scary horror story fast: you start at the end.

Yeah, you heard me right. Start at the end. Work backward. Figure out your story's climax, its final scare, that brutal moment when everything falls apart or the truth is revealed, and then reverse-engineer the entire thing. This isn't just a gimmick—it's how pros do it, how screenwriters structure their thrillers, and how you can build a horror story that doesn't meander but punches the reader straight in the gut.

Think about it like this: a horror story is a maze. If you don't know where the exit is, you're going to stumble around, get lost, backtrack, and probably give up. But if you know where the exit is—the ending—you can build a clear, terrifying path straight to it. Every twist, every scare, every character decision leads in that direction. That's how you keep your story tight, thrilling, and ultimately satisfying.

So how do you do it? Simple. You start by deciding what kind of ending you want. Is it a brutal, bloody climax where everyone dies? A shocking twist that flips the entire story on its head? A quiet, chilling reveal that sticks in the reader's mind long after they've closed the book? There's no right answer here. It's your nightmare—you get to decide how it ends.

Here's the beauty of working with ChatGPT. Once you have a vague idea of what you want the ending to be, you can use ChatGPT to help you flesh it out. You can literally type, "Give me ten possible climactic endings for a horror story about a cursed doll," and in seconds, you'll have a buffet of blood-curdling options. Some might be predictable. Some might be weird. But one or two of them will spark something in you, and suddenly you'll know exactly how your story ends.

Let's say, for example, you decide that your story ends with the protagonist locked in a burning house, realizing too late that the monster wasn't the ghost but something inside themselves. That's powerful. That's dark. That's your exit point. Now you can build the entire story backward from there. How did they end up in that house? What decisions led them to that moment? What scares and revelations had to happen along the way to make that ending hit hard?

This approach also makes plotting incredibly easy. Once you know the ending, you can break the story into clear, manageable chunks. You can use ChatGPT to help you structure the key beats: How does the protagonist first encounter the threat? What clues or warnings do they miss? What's the false hope moment? What's the final confrontation? You don't have to fumble in the dark because the ending is your flashlight.

Another reason this technique works so well, especially in horror, is that horror is all about payoff. You're building tension, dread, and fear for one reason—to deliver a punch at the end. If you don't know what that punch is, you're just piling up creepy scenes without a purpose. But when you start with the ending in mind, every scare has weight. Every moment of dread is leading somewhere. That's how you create a story that keeps readers glued to the page.

Here's where ChatGPT becomes an even more powerful co-writer. Once you've got your ending locked in, you can ask it to generate all the story elements you need to get there. You can say, "Outline a three-act horror story that leads to this ending." Or, "What obstacles would force my protagonist toward this ending?" You can even ask it to brainstorm red herrings, false scares, and side characters who will make the journey to that ending more intense.

The result is that you'll never sit there wondering, "What happens next?" You already know what happens next, because you know how it ends. You're just reverse-engineering the road to get there.

And here's another thing: starting with the ending actually makes your horror story scarier. Why? Because it lets you control the pacing and the buildup. You can strategically place scares, plot twists, and revelations so they build naturally toward that final moment. It keeps you from front-loading the horror and running out of steam halfway through. Instead, you're winding the tension tighter and tighter, so when the ending hits, it really hits.

It also helps you avoid one of the biggest problems amateur horror writers face—stories that fall apart in the third act. We've all read or watched horror stories where the setup is great, the middle is tense, but the ending is either too predictable or too chaotic to satisfy. That happens when writers don't plan the ending first. They write themselves into a corner and then scramble to find a way out. But when you start with the ending, there is no corner. You're guiding the story there from the very first line.

You can even use this technique to plant subtle clues, foreshadowing, and red herrings throughout the story. Because you know how it ends, you can leave breadcrumbs along the way—small, creepy details that won't make sense until the final reveal. That's how you write a horror story that rewards readers for paying attention, the kind of story that sticks in their heads long after they've finished.

Now, let's talk about a practical exercise you can do right now to lock in this mindset. Sit down and think about the scariest ending you can imagine. Don't worry about how you'll get there yet—just focus on the final image, the final twist, the final moment of dread. Is it your protagonist realizing they were the killer all along? Is it the monster smiling from the backseat as they drive away? Is it the final girl realizing she didn't survive after all?

Once you've got that ending, write it out. Describe it in vivid detail. Make it brutal, creepy, unexpected—whatever vibe you want. Then, and only then, start working backward. Ask yourself, "What had to happen to lead to this moment?" If you get stuck, bring in ChatGPT and ask for help filling in the blanks.

By the time you're done, you'll have the entire spine of your story laid out. And you'll be shocked at how quickly the writing flows when you know where you're headed.

In the next chapter, we're going to get into the nitty-gritty of horror story structure—how to take that ending you've just created and shape the beginning and middle around it, step by terrifying step. You'll learn how to build tension, stack scares, and keep your reader hooked until that final scream.

Because once you've got the ending, everything else is just walking backward through the dark.

The Basics of a Horror Story Structure

Now that you've got your ending locked in and you understand why working backward is the fastest, smartest way to build a horror story, it's time to talk about structure. Structure is the skeleton of your horror story. Without it, you're just throwing blood and shadows at the wall and hoping something sticks. But when you know how to structure a horror narrative, you can move quickly, hit all the right beats, and keep your reader squirming in their seat from the first page to the last.

The good news is that horror story structure isn't complicated. It's the same basic three-act structure used in every genre, but with one key difference: everything is designed to build tension, crank up the dread, and lead to that final terrifying payoff you've already created. So let's break it down and see how it works.

Act One is your setup. This is where you introduce the world, the characters, and the first signs that something is horribly wrong. You want to pull your reader in fast, give them a sense of normalcy, and then start chipping away at that normalcy until everything feels off. Think of it like the calm before the storm. Act One is where you plant the seeds of fear, even if the characters don't know it yet.

If your horror story is about a family moving into a creepy old house, Act One is where they're unpacking boxes, meeting the weird neighbors, and ignoring the strange noises in the attic. If your story is about a serial killer hunting college students, Act One is where you introduce the main characters and show their happy, clueless lives before the bodies start dropping.

But here's the thing—you don't want to waste time. In a one-day writing sprint, you need to get through Act One fast. Get the setup on the page, introduce your characters, give a hint of what's coming, and move on. ChatGPT can help you here. You can ask it to describe your setting in creepy detail, or to write a conversation between characters that subtly foreshadows the horror to come.

Act Two is where everything goes to hell. This is the middle of your story, the biggest chunk, and it's where the tension builds and builds until it's unbearable. In horror, Act Two is all about escalation. You start dropping scares, revealing the threat, and putting your characters in increasingly dangerous situations. Every scene should either increase the danger, raise the stakes, or reveal something new and terrifying about the threat.

This is also where you can play with pacing. Some scenes should move fast—a chase, an attack, a shocking death. Others should slow down and let the dread settle in—a character hearing whispers in the dark, finding a creepy message written on the wall, realizing they're being watched. You're controlling the reader's pulse here, speeding it up and slowing it down like a rollercoaster.

One thing to remember about Act Two is that it should feel hopeless. Your characters try to fight back, escape, or figure out what's going on, but nothing works. Every time they think they're safe, they're not. Every time they think they've figured it out, they haven't. The tension keeps rising until it feels like there's no way out.

Again, ChatGPT is your best friend here. You can use it to brainstorm creepy obstacles, plot twists, and terrifying imagery. If you get stuck, ask it to describe a nightmarish scene or to write a confrontation between your protagonist and the threat. It'll help you keep moving without getting bogged down.

Act Three is the climax and resolution. This is where everything comes crashing down. It's the final confrontation, the last scare, the moment when the protagonist either survives or dies, wins or loses, uncovers the truth or falls into madness. And because you already wrote your ending, you know exactly where this act is going.

The key to Act Three is payoff. You've spent the entire story building tension, dropping hints, and scaring the reader—now it's time to deliver. Don't hold back. Don't let the story fizzle out. This is where you go big, reveal the monster, kill off characters, unleash the twist, and leave the reader breathless.

Once the climax hits, you need to resolve the story quickly. Horror stories often end abruptly, with a final shock or a quiet, unsettling moment. You don't need to tie everything up neatly—in fact, horror works best when you leave the reader with lingering questions or a sense of unease.

Now, let's talk about one more crucial piece of horror structure: the turning points. These are the moments that change everything, that push the story forward and force the characters to act. You'll usually have one at the end of Act One, when the threat is revealed and the characters are forced to confront it. Another big turning point happens in the middle of Act Two, when the characters realize just how bad things really are. And the final turning point is the climax itself.

When you're writing your story in one day, knowing these turning points helps you stay on track. You don't have time to wander off into subplots or get lost in unnecessary details. You're moving from one key moment to the next, building tension with every step.

Here's a little trick I use when I'm writing fast: once I know my ending, I write a one-sentence summary of each turning point. Then I use ChatGPT to help me fill in the scenes that connect those points. It keeps me focused and helps me maintain the pace without losing steam.

One last thing to keep in mind about structure—don't be afraid to break the rules. Horror is the perfect genre for messing with expectations. You can flip the three-act structure on its head, start with the climax, or end on a cliffhanger. As long as you're building tension and delivering scares, you're doing it right. But having that basic structure in place—setup, escalation, climax—gives you a roadmap. It's the skeleton you hang the blood and guts on. It's how you make sure your story keeps moving and doesn't lose its way. And when you combine that structure with the speed and creativity of ChatGPT, you can write an entire horror story in one day without breaking a sweat. In the next chapter, we're going to dive into the heart of the horror story—the idea itself. You'll learn how to generate terrifying, original, and gripping horror story ideas fast, and how to use ChatGPT to help you unlock the darkest corners of your imagination.

Because before you can build your haunted house, you need to decide what kind of monster is living in it.

Finding Your Scariest Idea Fast

Let's be real for a second. The hardest part of writing anything—whether it's a horror story, a novel, or even a social media post—is figuring out what the hell you're going to write about. That blank page is scarier than any monster you'll ever create. But here's the good news: when it comes to horror, ideas are everywhere. Fear is universal, and the human brain is hardwired to react to it. You've got a lifetime of nightmares, creepy thoughts, childhood fears, and unsettling memories locked inside your head. You just need to shake them loose.

The key to writing a horror story in one day is not spending hours or days trying to come up with the "perfect" idea. You don't have time for that. You need an idea that's good enough to scare people, simple enough to build a story around, and strong enough to carry tension from start to finish. That's it. And you can find that idea in minutes if you know where to look—and how to use ChatGPT to help.

So, where do horror story ideas come from? Everywhere. Real life, urban legends, news headlines, old folk tales, fears you had as a kid, fears you have right now, even random thoughts that make your skin crawl. The trick is training yourself to think like a horror writer and recognize the dark potential in the ordinary.

Here's an easy exercise to get you started. Think about what scares you. Not what you think will scare other people—what scares you personally. Are you afraid of the dark? Of being followed? Of losing control of your body? Of something lurking under the bed? Of not knowing what's real and what's not? That's your starting point. Because if something scares you, chances are it will scare your readers too.

Once you've identified a fear, all you have to do is build a "what if" around it. What if the darkness wasn't empty, but alive? What if you were being followed—but no one else could see who was following you? What if your reflection started moving differently than you? That's how horror ideas are born. It doesn't have to be complicated. In fact, the best horror ideas are usually simple at their core.

Now, let's bring ChatGPT into the mix. This is where the process gets fast and fun. If you're staring at a blank screen, type something like, "Give me ten terrifying horror story ideas based on childhood fears." Or, "Generate five horror story premises about a haunted hotel." You can even narrow it down: "Give me horror story ideas where the monster is human, not supernatural." In seconds, you'll have a list of potential story seeds.

But don't stop there. Once you get a list, scan through it and see which one jumps out at you. Which one makes your stomach drop or gives you a little chill? That's the one you grab. And if none of them feel quite right, you tweak your request. Ask ChatGPT to make the ideas darker, more psychological, more violent, or more subtle—whatever flavor of horror you're craving.

Another great trick is to start with a real-life fear or phobia and ask ChatGPT to build a story around it. Afraid of elevators? Of deep water? Of being alone in a forest? Throw that at ChatGPT and ask, "What's the scariest story you can come up with about this?" It will start throwing ideas at you faster than your brain can keep up.

You can also pull inspiration from headlines and true crime. Horror thrives on the idea that the worst things often aren't monsters, but other people. Ask ChatGPT to take a true crime story and turn it into a fictional horror plot. Suddenly, you've got a terrifying, grounded idea that hits hard because it feels real.

Another fast way to generate a horror idea is to flip something familiar. Take a happy place and turn it dark. What if a child's teddy bear started whispering violent thoughts at night? What if a friendly neighbor was hiding something unspeakable in their basement? What if the place you go to feel safe—your home, your family, your own body—turned against you? Horror is at its most powerful when it corrupts the ordinary.

Here's something else to keep in mind. Your horror story idea doesn't need to be "original." There are no new ideas. Every horror story ever written is built on the same fears: death, loss, isolation, the unknown, being hunted, being powerless. What makes your story fresh isn't the core idea—it's how you execute it, how you twist it, how you make it personal. You could write yet another haunted house story, but if you fill it with specific, vivid, terrifying details and characters who feel real, it'll still scare the hell out of people.

That's where ChatGPT really helps. Once you've got a basic idea, you can ask it to brainstorm ways to make the story different. You can say, "How can I make this haunted house story feel fresh and unexpected?" Or, "What's a plot twist no one will see coming in this monster story?" Let ChatGPT do some of the heavy lifting while you stay focused on shaping the idea into something you're excited to write.

And don't get stuck thinking you need a huge, complex concept to write a great horror story. Some of the best horror is built on a single, terrifying idea. A videotape that kills you after you watch it. A man who can't wake up from his nightmares. A hitchhiker who disappears without explanation. Simple, punchy ideas are easier to execute, especially when you're writing fast.

Once you've landed on your scary idea, write it down in one sentence. Literally one sentence. Something like, "A woman trapped in an elevator slowly realizes she's not alone." Or, "A group of friends discover that the abandoned town they're exploring was never abandoned." That one sentence is your story seed. You can build everything else around it.

And here's the last, most important thing: once you've got your idea, commit to it. Don't waste time second-guessing yourself or wondering if it's good enough. It is. Your goal isn't to write the greatest horror story of all time in one day. Your goal is to write a complete, gripping, scary story that you can refine later. The idea just needs to get you started and keep you moving.

Because once you've got your scary idea, the real fun begins.

How to Choose the Right Horror Subgenre

So now you've got your scary idea. You've got something creepy, disturbing, chilling—or maybe downright gruesome—that you're excited to build a story around. But before you charge ahead and start writing, you need to make one more important decision: What kind of horror story are you writing? What's the flavor, the tone, the specific type of nightmare you're crafting?

In other words, what's your **subgenre**?

This might sound like a small thing, but choosing the right subgenre is the difference between writing a campfire ghost story or a psychological descent into madness. It shapes everything—the atmosphere, the pacing, the kind of characters you'll need, how the story escalates, and most importantly, what kind of fear you're trying to trigger in your reader.

Horror isn't just one thing. It's a whole haunted mansion of rooms, and each room has its own vibe. Let's walk through some of them so you can figure out which one fits your story idea best.

The first, and probably the most obvious, is **Supernatural Horror**. This is where you've got ghosts, demons, curses, witches, and all things otherworldly. If your idea involves haunted houses, possessions, or vengeful spirits, you're in the supernatural lane. These stories thrive on atmosphere, dread, and things that defy explanation. Think *The Conjuring*, *The Ring*, *Insidious*. If your idea has that "is this real or not?" flavor, or taps into the fear of something unseen but malevolent, supernatural horror is your playground.

Next up is **Psychological Horror**. This is where the real terror lives inside the characters' heads. The monster isn't always literal—it's the mind unraveling, paranoia, hallucinations, trauma, obsession. If your story revolves around unreliable narrators, descent into madness, or the blurred line between reality and nightmare, this is your subgenre. *The Shining*, *Black Swan*, *Jacob's Ladder*, and *The Babadook* live here. If your scary idea is about the protagonist slowly losing their grip, or realizing they're the monster, psychological horror is your jam.

Then you've got **Slasher Horror**. This is horror stripped down to its most brutal form. A killer, a body count, lots of tension and blood. The goal here is survival, the pace is fast, and the story thrives on action and violence. If your idea involves a masked murderer, a group of people being picked off one by one, or a final girl fighting for her life, you're writing a slasher. Think *Halloween*, *Friday the 13th*, *Scream*. It's simple, visceral, and very effective.

Another option is **Body Horror**. This is where the horror comes from physical transformation, mutilation, disease, or the grotesque. If your story involves someone's body turning against them, things growing inside them, or horrific experiments gone wrong, you're in body horror territory. Movies like *The Fly*, *The Thing*, and *Tusk* belong here. This is the subgenre for making readers squirm and wince at the sheer grossness of it all.

There's also **Folk Horror**. This one's about ancient traditions, rural settings, cults, pagan rituals, and the horrors that come from isolation and old belief systems. If your story idea involves small towns, creepy villages, or cult leaders with unsettling smiles, folk horror is your path. Think *The Wicker Man*, *Midsommar*, *The Ritual*. It's all about the clash between modern people and primal, ancient evil.

If your horror idea is more about mystery and investigation, you might lean toward **Horror Thriller** or **Mystery Horror**. These stories blend the tension of a thriller with horror elements. The protagonist is often trying to solve a crime or unravel a mystery, only to discover something terrifying. *Se7en*, *Silence of the Lambs*, and *The Others* all play in this space.

There's also **Survival Horror**. This is where the horror comes from an external, inescapable threat—whether it's monsters, natural disasters, or an apocalyptic scenario. If your idea is about characters trapped, hunted, or running out of options, this is your lane. Think *A Quiet Place*, *The Descent*, *28 Days Later*. It's all about tension, claustrophobia, and desperation.

And of course, there's **Cosmic Horror**—the kind made famous by H.P. Lovecraft. This is horror about the insignificance of humanity in the face of vast, unknowable forces. If your idea involves ancient gods, incomprehensible creatures, or people losing their minds trying to understand what they're up against, you're dabbling in cosmic horror. *The Mist*, *The Thing*, and *Event Horizon* are prime examples.

Finally, there's **Found Footage Horror** and **Mockumentary Horror**, where the story is told through video recordings, diary entries, or fake documentaries. This subgenre is all about realism and immersion, making the audience feel like they're discovering the horror themselves. If your idea is something that could be pieced together from lost tapes, you're in this category. Think *The Blair Witch Project*, *Paranormal Activity*, *Lake Mungo*.

So, how do you choose?

The best way is to ask yourself: **What's the scariest version of this idea?** Take your story seed and run it through the lens of each subgenre. Let's say your idea is: "A man discovers a mysterious door in his basement that wasn't there before." That's creepy already, but what's the scariest version?

If it's a supernatural horror, the door leads to a cursed dimension and something wants to get out.

If it's psychological horror, maybe the door isn't real—he's losing his mind.

If it's folk horror, the door is part of an ancient ritual.

If it's body horror, the door is growing inside him—literally.

If it's survival horror, the door traps him in a nightmare world with no escape.

You get the idea.

You can even ask ChatGPT to help you decide. Type something like, "What subgenre would make this horror idea scariest?" or "Rewrite this horror idea in the style of body horror." ChatGPT will instantly give you different angles to look at your concept and help you decide which one sparks the most excitement—or terror—in you.

Choosing your subgenre also helps you write faster because it gives you clear boundaries. Once you know what type of horror story you're writing, you know what tools to use. Supernatural horror leans into atmosphere and mystery. Slashers lean into action and violence. Psychological horror focuses on tension and character unraveling. You stop wasting time trying to make the story do everything, and instead laser-focus on doing one thing really, really well.

One last thing to remember: you can blend subgenres. Some of the best horror stories combine elements. *The Shining* is supernatural and psychological. *Alien* is cosmic horror and survival horror. *Hereditary* is folk horror and psychological. Don't be afraid to mix and match if it makes your story stronger. But pick a primary lane first. It'll make the writing process smoother and the story tighter.

Because once you know your subgenre, it's time to start scaring people.

Creating a Hook That Grabs by the Throat

If there's one thing you need to get right at the start of your horror story, it's the hook. Your hook is that first sentence, first paragraph, or first scene that reaches out of the page and grabs your reader by the throat, pulling them straight into the nightmare you've created. It's the thing that makes them stop scrolling, stop flipping, and say, "Okay, I have to know what happens next."

A weak opening kills a horror story before it even starts. Readers have short attention spans, and horror readers are even worse because they've seen it all—haunted houses, serial killers, creepy dolls. If your first few lines don't scream, "You're not safe here," they'll move on.

So how do you craft a hook that hits hard? You shock them. You confuse them. You disturb them. You intrigue them. Or you creep them out so badly they have no choice but to keep reading.

The first thing to understand about a good hook is that it doesn't waste time. You don't need to start with a long-winded description of the weather or a slow build-up of backstory. You don't need to explain how the protagonist grew up in a small town and had a distant relationship with their father. Not yet. In a horror story, your job is to slap the reader awake from the very first line. You want them uncomfortable immediately.

Think of your hook like the cold open of a horror movie. You know that scene before the title card where something awful happens to someone you don't even know yet? That's what you're aiming for. It's not about introducing the plot—it's about setting the tone and the tension.

There are a few ways to do this, and one of the fastest ways to generate killer hooks is to use ChatGPT. You can literally type, "Give me ten terrifying opening lines for a horror story about a haunted forest," and boom—you've got options. But let's talk about what makes a hook actually work.

One method is to open **in the middle of the horror.** Drop the reader right into the panic. Start with a scream, a body falling, a chase, a moment of chaos. This puts the reader off balance and immediately raises questions. Who's screaming? Why is there blood on the floor? Who's being chased? They won't stop reading until they get answers.

Another approach is to open with something **strange and unsettling.** Not outright terrifying—just... off. Maybe it's a line of dialogue that doesn't make sense, like, "The shadows in the corner keep whispering my name." Maybe it's an image that makes the reader pause, like, "On the third night, the wallpaper started bleeding." Something that nudges the reader and says, "Hey, something's not right here."

You can also open with **a question or a mystery.** Something that creates curiosity and dread at the same time. For example: "There were exactly thirteen teeth left on the doorstep, and none of them were hers." Now the reader is wondering, "Whose teeth? Why are they there? What's going on?" That's a hook.

Another powerful technique is to **hint at something bigger and more terrifying.** Start with a small, creepy moment and imply that it's just the beginning. "It started with the knocking in the walls, but that was before the voices came." That tells the reader, "You think this is bad? It's about to get worse."

And if you want to go dark fast, you can start with **death or violence.** Horror readers aren't squeamish—they expect blood. If your story opens with someone dying, someone discovering a body, or a moment of brutal violence, you immediately grab attention. But make sure it's not violence for shock's sake. It needs to serve the tone of your story and connect to the bigger horror you're about to unleash.

Here's something else to keep in mind: your hook should match the subgenre you've chosen. If you're writing psychological horror, your opening might be subtle, confusing, or surreal. If you're writing a slasher, you might start with a brutal murder. If it's supernatural, maybe it's a creepy encounter with something not quite human. The hook is your story's handshake—it tells the reader what kind of horror they're in for.

Now, let's talk about pacing. A good hook doesn't have to explain everything upfront. In fact, the best hooks raise questions without answering them. They create tension, not exposition. You want the reader leaning forward, needing to know more. Don't explain who the protagonist is, what town they live in, or what year it is. Give them just enough to feel scared, confused, or unsettled, and make them follow you to find out why.

And don't be afraid to rewrite your hook once the story's done. Often, the best opening lines come after you've written the ending and know exactly what the story is about. You can go back, sharpen that first sentence, make it hit even harder. Because in a horror story, the opening line isn't just an introduction—it's the first cut.

Let's look at a few examples of strong horror hooks and why they work:

"The thing under my bed keeps dragging me back when I fall asleep."

Simple, terrifying, raises questions. Why is there something under the bed? Why does it drag them back? What happens when they wake up?

"They buried her alive, and she hasn't stopped knocking since."

Immediate dread. You know something awful has happened, and you want to know how and why.

"I heard my mother's voice calling me from the kitchen. My mother died three years ago."

Classic ghost story hook. It's creepy, it's mysterious, and you instantly want to know what's happening.

Once you've got a few ideas, you can ask ChatGPT to punch them up. Say, "Rewrite this hook to make it scarier," or, "Give me five variations of this opening line." It'll give you options you might not have thought of, and one of them might be the perfect opening.

Your hook doesn't have to be poetic or literary. It doesn't need to be clever. It just needs to punch your reader in the gut and say, "You're not safe here. Keep reading."

Designing the Perfect Victim and Villain

You can't have a horror story without two key players—the victim and the villain. One exists to survive, the other exists to destroy. And if you want your horror story to hit hard and stay in your reader's head long after they've finished it, you need to design both of them so they feel real, memorable, and terrifying.

Let's start with the victim. In a horror story, the victim isn't just the person who dies first (although sometimes they are). They're the character your reader is supposed to care about, root for, or at the very least, watch with morbid fascination. They're the one who experiences the horror, and through them, the reader feels it too.

Here's the thing: a bland victim kills a horror story faster than the monster does. If your protagonist is a cardboard cut-out with no personality, no backstory, and no emotional depth, your reader won't care if they live or die. That's why the best horror stories give us victims who feel like real people. They have fears, flaws, relationships, and something to lose.

Start by asking yourself a few key questions:

What is this character most afraid of?

What do they want in life?

What's their biggest regret, their deepest secret, their softest spot?

You're not writing a biography here—you just need to know enough to make the reader invest. Maybe your protagonist is a single mother trying to protect her child. Maybe they're a grieving brother haunted by guilt. Maybe they're a skeptical journalist who doesn't believe in ghosts until they meet one. Whatever it is, give them something personal and specific. Horror hits hardest when it feels personal.

And don't make them perfect. Perfect characters are boring. Give them flaws—maybe they're selfish, or stubborn, or too curious for their own good. Their flaws should be part of why they end up in danger. The best horror stories are the ones where you can see the protagonist's choices dragging them deeper and deeper into the nightmare.

Now, let's talk about your villain. This is the fun part. Your villain is the engine of your horror story. They're the source of the dread, the fear, the blood, the body count. Whether it's a masked killer, a vengeful ghost, an ancient curse, or a creature from beyond the stars, your villain needs to be terrifying, but also interesting.

The biggest mistake writers make is creating a villain who's scary but empty. Sure, a guy with a knife and a mask can be creepy—but if that's all he is, your story won't stick. The best villains have layers. They have motives, backstories, rules, limits, and sometimes even a tragic reason why they're doing what they're doing.

Ask yourself:

What does your villain want?

Why are they doing this?

What's their connection to the protagonist?

And most importantly: What makes them scary?

Fear doesn't always come from violence. Sometimes it's the unknown—the thing you don't understand. Sometimes it's the villain's power, or their persistence, or the way they break the rules of reality. Sometimes it's the fact that they're human, and that's what makes them monstrous.

You can use ChatGPT to help you build your villain. Try prompts like, "Give me ten terrifying horror villains and their backstories," or, "Create a unique villain for a psychological horror story about isolation." ChatGPT can spit out ideas you might not have thought of, and you can mix and match elements to create something fresh.

Another thing to consider is the dynamic between victim and villain. The best horror stories aren't just about a killer and their prey—they're about a relationship. The victim and villain should be connected in some way, even if the victim doesn't know it at first. Maybe the villain is targeting the protagonist because of something they did in the past. Maybe they share a dark secret. Maybe the protagonist reminds the villain of someone they lost. Whatever it is, that connection makes the horror personal.

A great example of this is *It Follows*. The creature isn't just randomly attacking people—it's connected to the protagonist through a curse passed on by intimate relationships. That connection raises the stakes and makes the horror more meaningful.

Also, don't forget about the villain's **rules**. Every great horror villain has a set of rules, even if they don't make sense at first. Maybe the ghost only appears at midnight. Maybe the monster can't enter your home unless you invite it in. Maybe the killer leaves a mark on every victim. Rules make the villain scarier because they create a game your protagonist has to figure out—and if they break the rules, they die.

Once you've got your victim and villain designed, spend a little time imagining how they'll interact. How does the villain manipulate, hunt, or torment the victim? How does the victim fight back, or fail to fight back? Where's the tension? Where's the dread?

You can even use ChatGPT to simulate conversations or confrontations between them. Type, "Write a chilling scene where the protagonist confronts the villain for the first time," and see what comes back. It might give you a line of dialogue, a creepy visual, or an unexpected twist you can use in your story.

One more thing: your villain doesn't have to be a person. It can be a place, an idea, a force of nature, or even the protagonist's own mind. Psychological horror is filled with stories where the true villain is guilt, grief, or madness itself. If your horror story is more internal, make sure your "villain" still has clear traits, a presence that haunts the protagonist throughout the story.

In the end, your horror story works because of the relationship between victim and villain. The victim pulls the reader in emotionally; the villain keeps them on edge. It's a dance, a deadly game, a chase where one person's survival depends on understanding or escaping the thing that wants to destroy them.

In the next chapter, we're going to take all the characters, ideas, and subgenre choices you've made so far and show you how to plot a horror story in under an hour—a clear, step-by-step path from the hook to the ending.

Because now that you've built your monster, it's time to let it loose.

How to Plot a Horror Story in Under an Hour

Here's where things start to get real. You've got your terrifying idea. You've picked your subgenre. You've created a creepy villain and a relatable victim. You've even figured out how to hook your reader from the first sentence. Now it's time to connect all the dots and actually plot your horror story. And here's the best part—you can do it in under an hour.

Sounds impossible? It's not. In fact, with the system I'm about to show you and the help of ChatGPT, you'll wonder why you ever thought plotting a story had to be hard or time-consuming. It's all about breaking the process down into simple, manageable steps and trusting the horror structure we've already talked about.

First, you start at the end. Always. Remember, this whole book is about working backwards. You already know how your story ends—or at least, you should by now. You've got that final, horrifying moment locked in. Maybe your protagonist dies. Maybe they barely survive but are forever changed. Maybe they realize the monster was them all along. Whatever it is, you write it down clearly in one or two sentences. That's your destination.

Next, you need to figure out how the story begins. You want to open with your hook—the creepy, unsettling moment that pulls readers in. We talked about this in the last chapter. The opening should introduce your protagonist and the world they live in, but most importantly, it should plant the seed of fear. Maybe something small happens at first—a door creaks when it shouldn't, a stranger watches from across the street, a message appears on a mirror. Something that hints at the horror to come.

Once you've got your opening and your ending, you can map out the middle. This is where most writers get stuck because the middle of a story can feel like a swamp of possibilities. But not you. You're writing a horror story in one day, and you don't have time to get lost.

Here's how you do it: Break the middle of your story into three main beats.

First, the reveal. This is where your protagonist realizes something is wrong. They may not know the full extent of the horror yet, but the mask starts to slip. Maybe they see the villain's shadow. Maybe the body count starts. Maybe the ghost makes its presence known. Whatever it is, this is where the protagonist's normal world begins to fall apart.

Second, the escalation. Things get worse. Fast. The threat becomes undeniable, and your protagonist is in real danger. This is where you throw obstacles at them, crank up the tension, and raise the stakes. Maybe they try to escape and fail. Maybe they discover a terrible secret. Maybe the villain closes in.

Third, the point of no return. This is the moment when your protagonist has no choice but to confront the horror head-on. They've seen too much. They've lost too much. There's no running anymore. They either face the monster, or they die trying.

If you lay it out like this—opening hook, reveal, escalation, point of no return, and ending—you've basically got your entire plot mapped out. And here's the thing: You can do all of this in 20 minutes using ChatGPT.

You can literally type:

"Help me plot a three-act horror story about a man trapped in a haunted elevator. Here's how I want it to end: He realizes the elevator is a doorway to hell, and he's been dead the whole time."

And ChatGPT will spit out a full outline with all the beats in place.

Once you have that skeleton, you can go back and flesh it out. Add specific scenes, character moments, scares, twists. You can even ask ChatGPT to suggest creepy events for each act. For example:

"Give me five creepy events that happen in Act Two of this story."

You'll get a list of chilling possibilities to choose from.

And don't forget to add your villain's rules and behavior into the plot. If your villain only appears when the lights go out, make sure that rule shapes the plot. If the curse only activates when someone says a certain phrase, make that phrase matter. Rules keep the story tight and build tension.

One of the most powerful things you can do when plotting is to build cause and effect into every scene. In horror, every action has a consequence. If your protagonist ignores the warning signs, bad things happen. If they make the wrong choice, someone dies. If they confront the villain too early, it backfires. This chain of consequences keeps your story moving and keeps the reader on edge.

Another key element is pacing. Horror stories are like rollercoasters—you want to build tension, give the reader a quick scare, then let them breathe before you hit them again. Your plot should have peaks and valleys. Moments of high tension followed by brief, uneasy calm. That rhythm keeps the reader hooked and makes the scares hit harder.

And here's a pro tip: Always end your scenes with a question or a cliffhanger. Leave the reader needing to know what happens next. Horror is all about anticipation. The dread of what's coming is often scarier than the thing itself.

Let's do a quick recap of how you can plot your horror story in under an hour:

1. Write your ending first.
2. Write your opening hook.
3. Break the middle into three beats: reveal, escalation, point of no return.
4. Use ChatGPT to help fill in the gaps and brainstorm creepy events.
5. Make sure every scene leads logically to the next.
6. Build tension with pacing—peaks and valleys.
7. End scenes with questions or cliffhangers.

Once you've got this skeleton down, you can start writing. And because you already know where you're going and how to get there, the writing will flow fast. You're not wandering in the dark—you're racing toward the ending you've already planned.

In the next chapter, we're going to talk about how to build suspense like a master storyteller. Because a horror plot is only as good as the tension that holds it together—and I'm going to show you exactly how to keep readers on the edge of their seats.

Building Suspense That Keeps Readers Up at Night

If fear is the heart of horror, suspense is the pulse. You can have the scariest monster, the bloodiest deaths, and the creepiest setting—but if there's no suspense, your horror story will fall flat. Readers won't keep turning the page because gore alone isn't enough. It's the tension, the waiting, the sense that something awful is coming—that's what keeps people up at night, checking behind the shower curtain.

So how do you build suspense? How do you make your reader feel that tightness in their chest, that itch in the back of their brain, that rising panic that something terrible is about to happen?

It all comes down to how you control information, pacing, and anticipation. And luckily, you can do this easily and quickly—especially with ChatGPT riding shotgun.

Let's start with the golden rule of suspense: **The reader should always know just enough to be afraid, but never enough to feel safe.** You don't want to dump all the answers on them right away. You want to tease them, drip-feed them clues, and make them wonder what's really going on. Think of it like a horror movie trailer—show them flashes, hints, disturbing images, but never the full picture.

One of the fastest ways to create suspense is to **let the reader know something the protagonist doesn't.** This is called dramatic irony. It's when the reader sees the killer hiding in the closet, but the protagonist is brushing their teeth, unaware. It creates a delicious tension because the reader is screaming inside, "Don't open the door!" That's how you hook them.

You can also reverse it. Keep the reader in the dark and let the protagonist discover the horror in real time. This is especially effective in first-person or close third-person point of view, where the reader experiences every scare alongside the protagonist.

Suspense is also about pacing. You've probably heard that horror stories should be fast-paced—but that doesn't mean you have to rush every scene. In fact, slowing things down at the right moment can be even scarier. Let the reader sit in the tension. Describe the creaking floorboards, the shallow breaths, the way the shadows shift in the corner of the room. Make them feel trapped in that moment, just like your protagonist.

And when you do speed things up—when the chase begins, when the killer attacks, when the protagonist makes a run for it—it'll hit harder because you've built the tension first.

Another tool in your suspense-building kit is **unanswered questions.** Keep your reader guessing. What's making that sound in the attic? Why is the door locked from the outside? Who left the message scrawled in blood? Each question should lead to another, keeping the reader hungry for answers.

You can use ChatGPT to help you craft these moments. Ask it to suggest creepy questions, red herrings, or mysterious events that will keep your readers on edge. You can even type, "Give me ten suspenseful moments for a horror story about a cursed forest," and it will give you ideas to weave into your plot.

Foreshadowing is another essential ingredient. Drop hints early on that something bad is coming, but don't explain what. A broken mirror. A missing pet. A news report about unexplained disappearances. These little details build a sense of dread and make the reader uneasy, even when nothing scary is happening yet.

And don't forget about your setting. Horror settings aren't just backgrounds—they're characters. An abandoned hospital, a fog-covered forest, a crumbling Victorian mansion—all of them add to the suspense. Describe the details that make the place feel alive and dangerous. Use sensory language—sights, sounds, smells—to make the reader feel like they're there.

One of the most powerful ways to build suspense is to **make the reader care about the protagonist.** If your readers are emotionally invested, they'll be terrified when your protagonist is in danger. That's why you need to give your protagonist relatable fears, flaws, and desires. Make them human. The reader won't stay up at night worrying about a perfect hero—they'll worry about someone who feels real.

And here's something a lot of beginner horror writers miss: **Silence can be scarier than noise.** Don't fill every page with screams and action. Sometimes, the scariest moment is the quiet before the storm—the moment when nothing is happening, but the reader knows it's coming.

Another great technique is to create **false hope.** Let the protagonist (and the reader) believe they've found a way out, a solution, a safe place. Then pull the rug out from under them. That emotional whiplash heightens the suspense and keeps the reader guessing.

You can also use the "ticking clock" method. Put a time limit on the horror. Maybe the protagonist has until sunrise to survive. Maybe they have 24 hours to lift the curse. That countdown creates automatic tension because the reader knows the clock is always ticking.

And finally, don't be afraid to let the horror win. Not every horror story needs a happy ending. In fact, the best ones often don't. If the reader knows you're willing to kill off characters or let evil triumph, they'll never feel safe—and that's exactly what you want.

When you're writing your story, keep asking yourself:

What's the scariest thing that could happen next?

And if you're stuck, ask ChatGPT. Seriously. Type, "What's the most suspenseful thing that could happen in this scene?" or, "How can I make this moment tenser?" You'll get a list of options to choose from.

Remember, suspense isn't about shocking your reader over and over. It's about making them wait for the shock. It's about building tension so tightly that when you finally release it, it hits like a punch to the chest.

In the next chapter, we're going to dig into how to use ChatGPT specifically to generate twists and turns—those moments that flip the story on its head and make your reader gasp out loud.

Because suspense is great—but nothing beats a good twist.

Using ChatGPT to Generate Twists and Turns

Let's be honest—every horror story lives and dies by its twists. It's not just about monsters jumping out of closets or ghosts floating down hallways. The real, bone-deep scares come when the story flips on you, when everything you thought you knew is wrong, when the rug gets yanked out from under your feet and you're left staring at the truth with your mouth open and your heart racing.

A good twist doesn't just shock—it changes everything. It redefines the story you've been reading, makes you want to go back and see all the clues you missed, and leaves you thinking about it long after the lights are off.

The best part? You don't have to break your brain trying to come up with clever twists. You've got ChatGPT, and it's a plot-twisting machine if you know how to use it.

Here's how to do it.

The first step is to stop thinking about your story in a straight line. Horror stories shouldn't move neatly from Point A to Point B. They should zigzag, double back, and punch the reader in the gut when they least expect it. You've already mapped out your basic plot, but now it's time to mess with it.

A great way to start is by looking at your story from a distance and asking, "What's the obvious version of this story—and how can I destroy it?"

Let's say your plot is about a group of friends trapped in a haunted house. The obvious version is: The house is haunted, and the friends have to survive. Boring. So what if the house isn't haunted? What if one of the friends is setting them up? What if they're already dead and don't know it? What if the real horror isn't the house, but what's outside waiting for them when they try to leave?

Once you've got a few ideas, you can fire up ChatGPT and start playing.

Try typing:

"Give me ten plot twists for a horror story about a haunted house."

You'll get a list that includes everything from, "The ghosts are protecting the friends from something worse" to "The protagonist is the ghost and doesn't realize it." Some will be clichés. Some will spark something new in your brain. Either way, you're generating options fast, and one of them might be the twist your story needs.

Another approach is to ask ChatGPT to twist specific elements of your story. For example:

"What's an unexpected twist about the villain in this story?"

"How can I reveal that the protagonist is unreliable without giving it away too soon?"

"Give me a twist ending that leaves the reader unsettled."

ChatGPT will shoot back ideas like, "The protagonist realizes the villain was never real—it was a manifestation of their trauma," or "The final scene reveals the protagonist was the killer all along."

You can even ask for multi-layered twists.

"Give me a twist followed by a second twist that makes the first one even darker."

This is a great technique because readers love thinking they've figured it out—only to have the story flip again.

But here's the thing about twists: they only work if you set them up. You can't just pull a twist out of thin air at the end and expect it to land. You need to plant clues, hints, little details that seem harmless at first but make perfect, horrifying sense in hindsight.

This is where ChatGPT can help again. Once you've decided on your twist, you can ask:

"What clues can I drop early in the story to hint at this twist without giving it away?"

It'll give you a list of subtle foreshadowing techniques—strange dialogue, offhand comments, unsettling details—that you can sprinkle throughout your story.

Another thing to remember is that not all twists have to be huge, mind-blowing reveals. Some of the best horror stories are built on **small, creeping twists**—little shifts in what the protagonist knows or believes that slowly turn their world upside down. You can ask ChatGPT for these too.

"Give me five small but creepy twists for this horror story."

You'll get suggestions like, "The protagonist's reflection starts acting differently" or "A character's memories don't match the facts."

And don't be afraid to twist the reader's emotions. Make them sympathize with the villain. Make them question if the protagonist deserves to survive. Make them realize the horror is their fault. Horror isn't just about monsters—it's about revealing something dark, something uncomfortable, something you didn't want to see.

Let me give you an example of how this works in practice.

Say you're writing a psychological horror story about a woman who keeps hearing voices in her apartment. She thinks she's going insane. You can ask ChatGPT:

"What's a shocking twist for this story?"

You might get: "The voices aren't in her head—they're recordings planted by her neighbor."

Now you've got something juicy.

Next, ask:

"What clues can I plant early to hint at this twist?"

ChatGPT might suggest:

- The neighbor is always checking in on her at odd times.
- She finds an old tape recorder in her apartment and dismisses it.
- A strange delay when she hears the voices, like it's a recording.

Boom—you've just built a plot twist and the breadcrumbs leading to it in under ten minutes.

And here's a bonus trick: once you've written your story, you can ask ChatGPT to read it (paste the text) and suggest where you could add more twists or make the existing ones land harder. It's like having an editor who specializes in scaring the hell out of people.

But remember—twists aren't the goal. They're the spice. Your story still needs solid characters, a scary atmosphere, and a plot that makes sense. The twist is the knife in the dark, not the whole story.

In the next chapter, we're going to dig into the art of the scare itself—how to craft fear on the page, how to make your readers sweat, flinch, and keep the lights on while they read.

Because all the twists in the world won't save you if your story isn't actually scary.

The Art of the Scare: Crafting Fear in Words

Now we're getting into the meat of what makes horror tick—the scare itself. You can have the best twist, the creepiest villain, and a perfectly plotted story, but if you can't scare your reader in the moment, all of that falls flat. Horror readers aren't just looking for a good story; they're looking for an experience. They want to feel something crawling under their skin, make their heart pound, and force themselves to turn the page even when they really, really don't want to.

That's where the art of the scare comes in.

Writing something scary is a lot different than filming a jump scare or sneaking up behind someone and yelling "Boo!" You don't have the benefit of sound effects, visuals, or sudden shocks on the page. All you've got is language. But when you use that language well, words are more terrifying than any monster costume or horror movie soundtrack.

So, how do you actually craft fear in words?

The first thing to understand is that **fear is all about anticipation.** It's not the thing itself that's scary—it's the build-up to it. Think about every great horror scene you've ever read or watched. The scariest part isn't when the killer finally jumps out of the shadows. It's the moment right before, when the protagonist hears footsteps behind them, the door creaks open slowly, or they realize the lights won't turn back on.

You want to make your reader hold their breath, lean forward, tense up, waiting for something to happen. And when it does happen, you want them to feel it like a gut punch.

One of the fastest ways to build this kind of tension is to **slow the moment down.** When you're writing a scare, don't rush through it. Draw it out. Describe the little details—the sound of the character's breathing, the flicker of a shadow, the way the air feels heavier. Make the reader sit in the moment and squirm.

You can use sentence structure to help with this. Short, choppy sentences speed things up when the scare hits. Longer, winding sentences build tension and anxiety. Play with rhythm. Slow down when the tension is rising, then hit the reader fast when the scare drops.

Another powerful tool is **sensory detail.** Fear is a physical reaction, so engage the reader's senses. What does the room smell like? What does the character hear in the silence? How does their skin crawl, their stomach drop, their heart race? The more you make the reader feel like they're there, the more you pull them into the scare.

But don't overdo it. Too much description kills tension. You don't need a paragraph about how dusty the basement is—you need a sentence about how the dust dances in the beam of a flashlight, right before something moves in the darkness.

Uncertainty is your best friend. Fear thrives in the unknown. Don't show the monster right away. Don't explain everything. Let the reader wonder what's lurking behind the door, what's making that sound, what's really happening. Their imagination will always create something scarier than anything you can describe.

That's why implied horror is often more effective than explicit horror. A shadow at the edge of vision. A bloody handprint with no explanation. A half-heard whisper. Let the reader's brain fill in the blanks—and trust me, it will.

Another great technique is to **violate the reader's expectations.** Set them up to think they know what's coming, then flip it. Maybe the protagonist hears footsteps behind them, spins around—and there's nothing there. Relief. But then they turn back, and the thing is right in front of them. That emotional whiplash is what makes readers jump in their seats.

You can also use ChatGPT to help craft your scares. Seriously. If you're stuck, type:

"Describe a terrifying scene in a dark forest."

Or:

"Give me five creepy things that could happen in this abandoned hospital."

ChatGPT will give you a buffet of scary imagery, and you can pick and choose what fits your scene.

Another thing to keep in mind is that **fear is personal.** Not every scare will work on every reader. Some people are afraid of the dark, others of isolation, others of losing control. The best horror stories tap into universal fears—death, loss, the unknown—but also layer in specific, personal fears for the protagonist. When the reader connects to the character's fear, they feel it too.

That's why it's important to know your protagonist's deepest fear and use it against them. If they're afraid of being alone, isolate them. If they're afraid of losing a loved one, put that person in danger. If they're afraid of themselves, show them what they're capable of.

And here's something many horror writers forget: **Relief is part of the scare.** You can't keep the tension cranked up to eleven all the time. You need moments of quiet, of false safety, of breathing room. Because when the scare hits after that, it hits harder.

Think of it like pulling back a slingshot. The further you pull back—the more you lull the reader into feeling safe—the harder the shot when it finally fires.

Finally, don't be afraid to leave your reader unsettled. Horror isn't about tidy endings or clear answers. Sometimes, the scariest thing is what's left unsaid. End your scare scenes with a lingering sense of dread, an unanswered question, a feeling that something is still out there.

In the next chapter, we're going to dive into how to make your monster memorable—whether it's a ghost, a killer, or something far worse. Because once you know how to scare people, you need something (or someone) to deliver those scares.

How to Make Your Monster Memorable

Every horror story has its monster. It might be a literal beast with claws and fangs, a ghost that whispers in the dark, a masked killer stalking their prey, or something far more abstract—the creeping dread of isolation, the crushing weight of guilt, the inescapable presence of death itself. Whatever it is, your monster is the engine of your story's fear. It's the thing that keeps readers turning pages long after midnight.

But here's the thing: Not all monsters are created equal. Some horror stories leave you with a villain or entity you never forget—Freddy Krueger, Pennywise the Clown, the Xenomorph from *Alien*, even the nameless, shapeless thing in *The Blair Witch Project*. Others, well... you forget them before you've even closed the book.

If you want your horror story to stick, you need to make your monster memorable. And that's exactly what we're going to talk about in this chapter.

The first rule of creating a memorable monster is **giving it a clear identity.** Your monster can't be generic. It needs a defining feature, something specific and unique that sets it apart from every other ghost, ghoul, or serial killer out there. This could be physical—a disturbing appearance, an unusual weapon, a strange movement—or it could be psychological—a motive, a rule it follows, something it wants.

Think about what makes classic horror monsters unforgettable. Freddy Krueger has the clawed glove and the fact that he kills you in your dreams. Pennywise is a shapeshifting clown that feeds on fear. Michael Myers is an unstoppable, silent force who never runs but always catches you. Each one has something distinctive that etches them into your brain.

You can use ChatGPT to help you brainstorm here. Try typing:

"Give me ten unique horror monster concepts."

Or:

"What's a fresh take on a haunted house entity?"

You'll get a list of creepy, creative ideas you can riff on.

The next thing to focus on is **your monster's rules.** Every great horror villain operates by a set of rules—even if they're supernatural or unknowable. Maybe your monster can't cross running water. Maybe it only appears when someone breaks a specific taboo. Maybe it can't hurt you unless you look at it. These rules not only make your monster interesting—they make your story more suspenseful. The protagonist has to learn the rules to survive, and the reader gets to piece them together along the way.

Rules also help your monster feel real. Even the most surreal or cosmic horror becomes scarier when it has boundaries because it feels like something that could exist within the story's world.

Another trick to making your monster stick is to give it a **backstory.** It doesn't have to be long or complicated, but readers love a monster with a tragic or terrifying origin. Maybe the ghost was betrayed and murdered. Maybe the killer was shaped by childhood trauma. Maybe the monster is the result of something the protagonist did—or failed to do.

That backstory gives weight to the horror. It creates sympathy, or at least understanding, and makes the scares hit harder because there's something human buried under all that terror.

You can even use ChatGPT to flesh this out. Try:

"What's a disturbing backstory for a horror villain who haunts an abandoned motel?"

You'll get creepy, unexpected ideas you can weave into your plot.

Appearance matters too. You want your monster to be visually striking—not just so readers can picture it, but so the image sticks in their minds. That doesn't mean it has to be grotesque (although it can be). Sometimes, the simplest, eeriest visuals are the ones that last. Think of the girl in *The Ring* with her long black hair covering her face. Simple. Iconic. Terrifying.

When you describe your monster, focus on the sensory details that make it unsettling. How does it move? What does it smell like? What does it sound like? How do people feel when they're near it? Readers might forget what your monster looks like, but they'll never forget how it made them feel.

Another way to make your monster memorable is to **tie it to a theme.** The best horror monsters aren't just scary—they mean something. They represent a fear, an idea, a trauma. In *It Follows*, the monster represents the fear of intimacy and consequences. In *The Babadook*, the monster is grief and depression. In *A Nightmare on Elm Street*, Freddy is the embodiment of guilt and fear passed down by parents' sins.

Ask yourself: What does your monster symbolize? Is it about fear of death? Fear of losing control? Fear of the past catching up to you? Once you know, you can weave that meaning into the story and make your monster more than just a scare—it becomes unforgettable.

Finally, and this is important: **Make your monster active.** Don't let it sit in the shadows too long. Horror stories are about tension and fear, but they're also about conflict. Your monster should be hunting, stalking, manipulating. It should have agency. A horror villain who waits around isn't scary. A horror villain who's always one step behind you—or worse, one step ahead—is terrifying.

And here's a bonus tip: If you want to make your monster even more disturbing, give it a **voice.** Not literally, necessarily. But give it personality. Let it taunt, whisper, manipulate, or leave messages. Make it personal. The more your monster engages with the protagonist, the more real and terrifying it becomes.

You can even use ChatGPT to help you write these moments. Ask:

"Write a creepy message a horror villain might leave for the protagonist."

You'll get a handful of spine-chilling options to drop into your scenes.

At the end of the day, your monster is the beating, black heart of your horror story. It's what your readers will remember when they close the book and try to sleep. So make it specific, make it scary, give it rules and backstory, tie it to something deeper—and let it loose.

Setting the Scene: Horror Locations That Terrify

You can have the best hook, the scariest villain, and a plot packed with tension, but if your setting is weak, your horror story is going to fall flat. The location in a horror story isn't just a backdrop—it's a character in itself. It breathes. It watches. It traps. It haunts. When you do it right, the setting creates unease before anything actually happens. It primes your reader's fear sensors and keeps them unsettled from start to finish.

So let's talk about how to set the scene in a way that terrifies.

First, you've got to understand why location matters so much in horror. It's all about **control and isolation**. Horror settings work best when the environment itself is dangerous, unfamiliar, or inescapable. The classic examples: an abandoned asylum, a dark forest, a haunted house, an empty school at night, a desolate motel on the edge of nowhere. These places work because they strip your characters of safety. There's no help coming. There's no one around to hear them scream.

Your location should make your protagonist—and your reader—feel trapped.

The second reason setting is so important is because it sets the **tone and atmosphere**. A bright, bustling city street isn't scary. But that same street at 3 a.m., empty and echoing with footsteps behind you? That's terrifying. The location shapes the mood. It tells the reader how they should feel before the first scare even happens.

When you're writing your horror story, ask yourself:

Where's the worst possible place for this nightmare to unfold?

And don't just settle for the obvious. Sure, abandoned hospitals and creaky mansions are great, but you can make almost any location scary if you build it right.

A suburban house can be terrifying if it feels like something's watching from the closet. A public park can be unsettling if it's empty and silent when it shouldn't be. Even a cheerful carnival can turn nightmarish when the lights go out and the music keeps playing.

Once you've picked your setting, it's time to bring it to life. And this is where your words—and ChatGPT—come in handy.

Start by focusing on **sensory detail.** Make the reader feel like they're there. Describe the smell of mold and old wood in the haunted house. The sound of dripping water in the underground tunnel. The way the cold, damp air sticks to the protagonist's skin. Don't just say "the forest was creepy." Show it: "The trees leaned too close, their twisted branches clawing at the sky, blocking out the moon."

You can ask ChatGPT to help you with this. Try typing:

"Describe a terrifying abandoned hospital in vivid detail."

You'll get a paragraph that paints the scene, and you can tweak it to fit your story.

But don't just describe the setting—**make it active.** The best horror locations feel alive. They creak, groan, shift in the darkness. They hide things. They manipulate the characters. Your setting should be more than a static backdrop—it should feel like it's working against your protagonist.

Think about how the setting can affect the plot. Maybe the protagonist gets lost in a maze of identical hallways. Maybe the house rearranges itself when no one's looking. Maybe the forest never ends, no matter how far they run. Use the location as an obstacle, a trap, a source of tension.

And don't forget to tie the setting to the story's theme or monster. If your story is about psychological horror, maybe the setting is a crumbling old house that mirrors the protagonist's fractured mind. If it's about isolation, set it somewhere remote—a cabin in the woods, a boat in the middle of the ocean, a space station orbiting a dead planet.

Your setting should reflect the horror. It should amplify the protagonist's fear, not just physically but emotionally.

Here's another trick: **Start normal, then make it strange.** One of the most unsettling ways to use setting in horror is to take a familiar place and make it feel wrong. A school after dark. An empty shopping mall. A quiet street at dawn. You don't have to invent a gothic castle—you just have to twist the ordinary into something uncomfortable.

The uncanny is powerful. When something is almost normal but slightly off, it creeps under the reader's skin. A flickering streetlight. A playground swing moving on its own. A house where all the family photos have the eyes scratched out. These little details create a mood that sticks with the reader long after the story's done.

And here's a pro tip: **Use weather and time of day to your advantage.** Horror stories love storms, fog, darkness, cold. But you can also flip the script and make something scary happen in broad daylight. There's something deeply unsettling about a horror story that refuses to hide in the dark.

Let's not forget sound. You're writing words, but that doesn't mean you can't use sound to scare your reader. Describe the distant knock, the whisper in the vents, the scrape of something moving just out of sight. Make your setting noisy in the worst possible way.

And when you're stuck, ChatGPT is right there to help. You can type:

"Give me ten creepy things about an abandoned hotel."

Or:

"Describe the scariest thing that could happen in a cornfield at night."

You'll get a list of atmospheric details you can sprinkle throughout your story.

The key is to make your setting part of the horror, not just the backdrop. Your protagonist shouldn't just be running from the monster—they should feel like the walls are closing in, the shadows are reaching out, the whole world is conspiring against them.

Writing a Strong Protagonist in a Horror Story

You might think horror stories are all about the monster, the setting, or the scares—but here's the truth: none of it matters if your protagonist is boring. Readers won't care how creepy your villain is or how terrifying your world feels if they don't care about the person trying to survive it. Your protagonist is the audience's anchor. They're the one who bleeds, breaks, runs, fights, screams, and maybe, just maybe, survives.

So, if you want your horror story to hit hard, you need to write a strong protagonist. Not necessarily strong in the action-hero sense—sometimes they're fragile, broken, or deeply flawed—but strong in that they feel real, layered, and human.

Let's start with the basics. Your protagonist should have something to lose. Horror only works if there's something at stake beyond their physical survival. Maybe it's their sanity. Maybe it's their family. Maybe it's their freedom, their guilt, their soul. If your protagonist is a blank slate with nothing to lose, the reader won't feel the tension.

One of the fastest ways to build a solid protagonist is to give them a **fear**—something specific, something personal, something that shapes how they react to the horror around them. And I'm not just talking about fear of the monster. I mean something deeper. Fear of abandonment. Fear of losing control. Fear of becoming like their abusive parent. Fear of being powerless.

Once you know that fear, you can design your story to poke at it over and over again. The monster becomes an external representation of the protagonist's internal terror. That's how you make your story resonate on a deeper level.

You can use ChatGPT to help you flesh this out. Type:

"Give me five deep, personal fears for a horror story protagonist."

You'll get options like fear of isolation, fear of being forgotten, fear of hurting someone they love—and you can choose one that fits your story.

Next, make your protagonist **flawed.** Perfect characters don't belong in horror stories. They're not believable, and worse, they're not interesting. Readers connect to flaws because they see themselves in them. Maybe your protagonist is selfish, stubborn, cowardly, reckless. Maybe they're running from something they did. Maybe they're in denial about what's happening.

Those flaws should get them into trouble. They should make bad decisions. They should push people away. They should hesitate at the worst possible moment. Because in horror, the scariest thing isn't always the monster—it's the human capacity to screw things up.

But here's the key: even with all their flaws, your protagonist needs to be **sympathetic.** The reader doesn't have to like them, but they do have to root for them. Give them a goal, a relationship, a moment of vulnerability. Show them fighting to survive, to save someone else, to do the right thing even when it's hard.

One way to do this is to show your protagonist's **growth.** The best horror protagonists change over the course of the story. They start out afraid, broken, unsure—and by the end, they've been hardened, damaged, or transformed. Sometimes they survive. Sometimes they don't. But they're never the same.

Think about classic horror protagonists. Laurie Strode in *Halloween* starts as an innocent babysitter and ends up fighting for her life, forever changed by what she's witnessed. Wendy Torrance in *The Shining* goes from terrified wife to fierce protector. Clarice Starling in *The Silence of the Lambs* starts as a rookie agent and ends up facing her worst fears.

That arc—the hero's journey twisted into a nightmare—is what keeps readers invested.

And don't forget: **Your protagonist drives the plot.** Horror stories can easily become passive—a series of things happening to the characters. But a strong protagonist makes choices. They investigate the creepy sound. They decide whether to run or fight. Their actions move the story forward and create the tension.

You can use ChatGPT to map this out, too. Try:

"Outline a character arc for a horror protagonist who is terrified of being alone."

It will give you a step-by-step breakdown of how your protagonist can grow, change, and react to the horror around them.

Another important thing to keep in mind is **perspective.** Horror works best when it's intimate, when the reader experiences every fear, doubt, and breath alongside the protagonist. Whether you're writing in first-person or close third-person, you want the reader to see the world through your protagonist's terrified eyes.

That doesn't mean you have to reveal everything. In fact, the best horror stories use the protagonist's limited knowledge to build suspense. Let them misinterpret what's happening. Let them miss the signs. Let them unravel slowly. The reader should feel like they're trapped in the nightmare with them.

Your protagonist's voice matters, too. Whether they're calm and rational, panicked and scattered, bitter and cynical, or broken and numb, their personality should bleed through every line of narration. A horror story isn't just about what happens—it's about how the protagonist experiences it.

Finally, don't be afraid to let your protagonist lose. Horror is one of the few genres where the hero doesn't always win. Sometimes they die. Sometimes they escape but are scarred forever. Sometimes they realize they were the villain all along. A strong protagonist doesn't mean a victorious protagonist—it means someone the reader will never forget, even if they don't survive.

In the next chapter, we're going to talk about how to create a truly sinister antagonist—because now that your protagonist is ready to suffer, you need a villain worthy of the job.

How to Create a Sinister Antagonist with ChatGPT

Now that you've crafted a strong, flawed, and relatable protagonist, it's time to make their life a living nightmare. And to do that, you need a proper villain—a sinister, unforgettable antagonist who drives the terror, manipulates the tension, and keeps both your protagonist and your reader looking over their shoulder.

In horror, the antagonist is more than just "the bad guy." They are the fear. They are the dread that creeps in slowly and the thing that jumps out at you in the dark. Whether your antagonist is a monster, a ghost, a serial killer, or something much more abstract, their job is to actively generate terror and conflict.

But here's the thing—you don't have to come up with all of this on your own. You've got ChatGPT in your corner, and if you use it right, it can help you build a villain who will crawl under your reader's skin and stay there long after the story's done.

So, how do you create a truly sinister antagonist?

It starts with asking the right questions. And ChatGPT is perfect for this. Try something like:

"Give me ten unique, terrifying antagonist ideas for a psychological horror story."

Or:

"What would be a disturbing backstory for a supernatural horror villain?"

You'll immediately get options that range from classic horror fare to totally off-the-wall ideas you wouldn't have thought of on your own. Pick the one that makes you feel a little uncomfortable—that's your villain.

But don't stop at just an idea. A memorable horror antagonist needs three key things: **motive, method, and presence.** And ChatGPT can help you flesh out each one.

Let's break it down.

Motive:

Why is your antagonist doing what they're doing? Even the most monstrous villains have a motive. It might not make sense to anyone but them, but it drives them. Maybe they want revenge. Maybe they're cursed. Maybe they're trying to fill an emptiness inside themselves. Maybe they're feeding on something—fear, flesh, souls.

The more personal and twisted the motive, the better. You can prompt ChatGPT with:

"Give me five disturbing motives for a horror antagonist."

You'll get answers like:

- They believe they're saving people by killing them.
- They're trapped in a time loop and must kill to escape.
- They're punishing others for sins they committed themselves.

Choose one that fits the tone of your story, or mix a few together to create something even darker.

Method:

How does your antagonist operate? What makes them terrifying isn't just what they want—it's how they get it. Are they quiet and manipulative? Brutal and unstoppable? Do they follow a specific pattern or set of rules? Do they leave messages, trophies, or marks?

Method is how you control the pacing and fear in your story. You want your readers to wonder what the antagonist will do next—and when they'll strike.

Ask ChatGPT for help:

"Describe five terrifying methods an antagonist could use to stalk their victim."

You'll get chilling suggestions like:

- Leaving cryptic, personal messages in the protagonist's home.
- Appearing only in reflections, never in person.
- Slowly turning people in the protagonist's life against them.

Presence:

This is the intangible quality that makes your antagonist stick in your reader's mind. It's how they make the reader feel. A good horror villain isn't just scary when they're on the page—they're scary when they're not. They linger. Their shadow stretches across the entire story.

You create presence through the reactions of your characters. Show how terrified, obsessed, or broken the protagonist becomes because of the antagonist. Build the antagonist's legend. Let side characters whisper about them. Let their reputation loom over every scene, even when they're not physically there.

If you want to take it even further, give your antagonist a **voice.** Let them taunt, manipulate, or even charm the protagonist. Dialogue with a villain can be some of the most unsettling parts of a horror story. And again, you can use ChatGPT to help:

"Write a chilling conversation between a horror protagonist and their villain."

You'll get dialogue dripping with tension that you can weave right into your story.

Here's a little secret: The scariest antagonists aren't always supernatural. Sometimes, they're people. People with broken minds, warped morals, or nothing left to lose. Sometimes, they're the protagonist themselves—the darkness inside them, the guilt they can't shake, the consequences of their own actions.

You can use ChatGPT to brainstorm those kinds of antagonists too:

"Give me five ideas for an internal antagonist in a psychological horror story."

And don't forget, your antagonist doesn't have to be seen to be scary. Sometimes the best horror villains are unseen forces. A curse. A disease. A presence that can't be touched or reasoned with. You can use ChatGPT to help you build those intangible horrors as well.

Once you've got your antagonist fully formed—motive, method, presence—tie them directly to your protagonist. The best horror stories make the villain personal. Maybe the antagonist is a reflection of the protagonist's worst fear. Maybe they share a traumatic past. Maybe the antagonist is the consequence of something the protagonist did or failed to do. That connection creates real tension and stakes.

Before you move on, here's a quick exercise you can do with ChatGPT. Type:

"Create a detailed profile for a horror antagonist who is hunting the protagonist because of a past betrayal."

You'll get back a villain with a backstory, personality, methods, and motive you can drop straight into your plot.

The Psychology of Fear and How to Tap Into It

If you really want to scare your reader, you can't just throw blood, guts, and jump scares at them. Anyone can write about something spooky happening in the dark. But to truly crawl under someone's skin—to keep them thinking about your story long after they've finished reading—you need to understand fear itself. You need to tap into the deep, primitive psychology of why we get scared in the first place.

So let's break it down. What is fear?

At its core, fear is survival instinct. It's your brain reacting to a threat, whether that threat is real or imagined. Fear is what kept our ancestors alive when there were predators lurking outside the cave. It's why our senses heighten in dangerous situations, why our heart races, why we freeze, run, or fight. It's built into our DNA.

And horror stories? They're engineered to poke at that primal instinct over and over again.

But here's the trick: Fear is personal. What scares one person might not scare another. Some readers are terrified of ghosts and demons. Others are scared of being alone, losing control, or going insane. That's why the best horror stories don't rely on just one type of scare—they layer fears, psychological and physical, until the reader can't breathe.

So how do you use this in your story?

You start by identifying **universal fears.** These are the things almost everyone is afraid of on some level. Death. The unknown. Pain. Loss. Isolation. Helplessness. Betrayal. These fears are hardwired into the human experience, which means they're powerful tools for any horror writer.

Then you layer in **personal fears.** These are the fears specific to your protagonist—and, by extension, your reader. Fear of being abandoned. Fear of hurting someone they love. Fear of the past catching up to them. Fear of what's hiding inside their own mind. These fears make the horror feel intimate and unique.

For example, imagine a horror story about a haunted house. The universal fear is easy: ghosts, death, things that go bump in the night. But what if the protagonist is also terrified of being alone? Suddenly, every creaking floorboard and whisper in the dark hits harder because it's poking at their deepest, most personal fear.

You can use ChatGPT to help identify these fears. Try typing:

"List ten deep psychological fears that can be used in a horror story."

You'll get options like fear of losing identity, fear of being trapped, fear of being watched—all of which can fuel your narrative.

Another way to tap into the psychology of fear is to understand **how fear builds.** It's not just about the monster jumping out at you—it's about the anticipation, the dread, the creeping sense that something is wrong. Fear builds in stages:

Discomfort → Unease → Dread → Panic → Terror

Your job as the writer is to walk the reader through those stages. Start with something small—something out of place, something unsettling. Then escalate. Tighten the tension. Make the protagonist doubt themselves. Make the reader question what's real. And when they're at their most vulnerable, hit them with the real horror.

You can also use **uncertainty** to trigger fear. The human brain hates not knowing. That's why horror works so well when you leave things unexplained. What's making that noise? Why did the lights flicker? What's lurking in the shadows? The moment you explain too much, the fear often fades. Let your reader fill in the blanks with their own imagination—that's where real terror lives.

A technique many horror writers use is called **the uncanny.** It's when something is almost normal, but slightly off. A doll that looks too lifelike. A reflection that moves a second too late. A smile that's just a little too wide. The uncanny taps into the brain's survival instinct—it knows something's wrong, but it can't quite figure out what.

You can ask ChatGPT to help you generate uncanny details:

"Describe five unsettling, uncanny things that could happen in a horror story."

You'll get ideas you can drop into your scenes to keep readers on edge.

Isolation is another powerful psychological trigger. When the protagonist is cut off—from help, from information, from other people—their fear intensifies. The setting can help with this. An abandoned building. A remote cabin. A deserted town. Even a crowded city can feel isolating if no one believes the protagonist or if everyone they trust disappears.

And let's not forget **loss of control.** One of the deepest human fears is losing control—of the situation, of the environment, of your own mind. That's why psychological horror is so effective. When the protagonist starts doubting what's real, when they can't trust their own senses, the reader feels that panic too.

You can also tap into **moral fears.** The fear of doing something unforgivable. The fear of becoming the monster. The fear of crossing a line you can't uncross. These themes create horror that lingers, horror that stays with the reader because it's rooted in human weakness, not just external threats.

And don't underestimate the power of **anticipation.** Fear isn't just about what happens—it's about what might happen. Your readers should always feel like the monster is one step away, even when nothing is happening. Create a constant sense of threat, a feeling that something is about to go horribly wrong.

One practical way to keep this tension is to plant questions and never answer them immediately. Why is the door locked from the outside? What's buried in the backyard? Why does the protagonist's reflection look different? Let the reader squirm while they wait for the answers.

ChatGPT can help you keep the tension high. You can type:

"What unanswered questions can I plant in a horror story to keep readers uneasy?"

You'll get a list of creepy mysteries you can weave into your plot.

At the end of the day, the psychology of fear comes down to one thing: **loss of safety.** Readers read horror to feel unsafe, to explore the darkness from the comfort of their chair. Your job is to create that darkness, step by terrifying step.

Dialogue That Chills: Letting Characters Sound Real

If there's one thing that can instantly kill the tension in a horror story, it's bad dialogue. You can build the creepiest atmosphere, craft a brilliant antagonist, and plot the scariest twists—but if your characters talk like cardboard cut-outs, the reader is going to roll their eyes instead of gripping the page. Dialogue is where your characters become real. It's where your horror story breathes. And when you get it right, it's where you can deliver some of the most chilling, unsettling moments in the entire narrative.

So let's talk about how to make your dialogue not just believable—but terrifying.

First, and this is key, **characters in a horror story should sound like real people.** That means their conversations should feel natural, grounded, and specific. Too many horror stories fall into the trap of having characters deliver stiff exposition or unrealistic, polished lines. Real people stumble, interrupt each other, swear, joke to hide fear, or trail off when they're terrified.

Think about how people talk when they're scared. They don't deliver long, poetic speeches. They panic. They whisper. They argue. They gasp for breath. Sometimes they say nothing at all. Silence can be the most powerful line in your entire story.

You can use ChatGPT to help make your dialogue more authentic. Try typing:

"Write a realistic, tense conversation between two characters trapped in a haunted house."

You'll get a back-and-forth exchange full of fear, doubt, and human emotion that you can adapt and refine.

Another thing to watch out for is **exposition dumps.** Horror readers want to feel the fear, not have it explained to them in a five-minute monologue. If you need to deliver information, do it naturally—through arguments, desperate whispers, journal entries, or cryptic warnings from other characters. Make the dialogue part of the action, not a break from it.

One of the best ways to make dialogue chilling is to use it to **reveal fear.** Let your characters' personalities come through in how they react to the horror around them. One character might crack jokes to hide how scared they are. Another might shut down and say almost nothing. Another might ramble, talk too much, say the wrong thing because they're unraveling.

Use their words—or lack of words—to show how the horror is affecting them.

You can also use dialogue to **build suspense.** Have characters interrupt each other. Let one character try to confess something important, only to get cut off by a noise outside. Drop half-finished thoughts, ominous warnings, whispered threats. The more incomplete and uncertain the dialogue, the more tension you create.

And don't forget the power of a well-placed **creepy line.** A single sentence can stick in the reader's brain like a splinter. Think of classics like *The Sixth Sense's* "I see dead people." You don't need to overdo it—one or two chilling lines in the right place can make the entire story feel more unsettling.

ChatGPT is a goldmine for this. You can type:

"Give me ten creepy lines a horror villain might say to the protagonist."

You'll get lines that make your skin crawl, and you can sprinkle them throughout your story for maximum effect.

Another great way to use dialogue in horror is to play with **ambiguity.** Let characters say things that can be interpreted multiple ways. A neighbor says, "You shouldn't stay here after dark," but won't explain why. A child says, "The man in the closet told me you're next." Dialogue like this plants seeds of doubt and dread in the reader's mind.

Foreshadowing through dialogue is also powerful. Let your characters drop small, ominous hints early on that won't make sense until the climax. A line like, "It's not the dark you should be afraid of," hits differently when the protagonist realizes the monster only appears in daylight.

And remember, not every character needs to talk the same way. **Voice matters.** Your characters should sound different based on who they are. A frightened child won't speak like a jaded detective. A grieving parent won't talk like a clueless teenager. When you make each voice distinct, the world feels more real—and the fear hits harder.

One trick I use when writing dialogue is to actually **read it out loud.** If it sounds stiff, awkward, or too polished, I rewrite it. You want it to sound like something a real person would say in that situation.

If you get stuck, ask ChatGPT to help you punch up a conversation. Try:

"Rewrite this dialogue to make it more tense and realistic."

You'll be surprised how quickly you can transform a flat scene into one crackling with dread.

Another way to use dialogue to your advantage is through the **villain's voice.** Whether your antagonist is a masked killer, a ghost, or something far worse, giving them a distinct way of speaking can make them ten times scarier. Maybe they never raise their voice. Maybe they mimic the voices of their victims. Maybe they speak in riddles, or calm, measured threats.

You can even have the villain's dialogue reveal their backstory or motive without a big info dump. A casual, chilling comment like, "I remember how you screamed last time," tells the reader everything they need to know without spelling it out.

And don't underestimate the power of **silence.** Sometimes the most chilling dialogue is what isn't said. A character trailing off mid-sentence. A radio crackling to life with static instead of words. A voicemail with only breathing on the other end. Horror is as much about what's missing as what's present.

How to Use ChatGPT for Atmospheric Descriptions

If horror is a dark ride, atmosphere is the creaking track beneath it. You can have a great plot, terrifying villain, and strong characters—but without atmosphere, your horror story feels empty. The atmosphere is what wraps around the reader like cold air, what makes their skin prickle even when nothing's happening. And the good news? You don't have to spend hours agonizing over crafting those chilling descriptions. You've got ChatGPT in your toolkit, and when used right, it can help you build an atmosphere so thick and oppressive, your reader will feel like they're right there in the middle of your nightmare.

So, let's talk about how to use ChatGPT to generate atmospheric descriptions that elevate your horror story without slowing it down or sounding overdone.

First, you need to understand **what atmosphere is.** It's not just about describing things. It's about creating a mood. Atmosphere is the vibe of your story—it's the dread, the unease, the claustrophobia, the creeping sense that something is very wrong. You build it by describing sights, sounds, smells, textures, even temperature. It's the sensory backdrop that supports your horror.

The fastest way to use ChatGPT to generate this is by feeding it specific prompts. For example:

"Describe an abandoned hospital at midnight in a chilling, atmospheric way."

Or:

"Write a creepy, sensory description of a dark forest where something is watching."

What you'll get back is a block of descriptive text loaded with sensory detail and mood.

But don't stop there. Once ChatGPT gives you a draft, refine it. Cut what you don't need. Tighten the language. Make sure it sounds like **your voice**—don't let it sound too flowery or overwritten unless that fits your style.

The goal is to sprinkle this atmosphere throughout your story, not dump it in big chunks that slow down the pacing. One or two creepy sensory details per scene is often enough to keep the reader uncomfortable without distracting them.

Another trick is to use ChatGPT for **micro-atmosphere moments.** Instead of asking for an entire location description, ask for a specific unsettling detail:

"What's one creepy thing about an empty playground at night?"

ChatGPT might come back with something like: "The rusted swing creaks back and forth in the wind, even though there's no breeze."

That's gold. You can drop a line like that anywhere in your story to instantly amp up the atmosphere.

You can also use ChatGPT to help you vary your atmospheric descriptions so they don't all sound the same. Try prompts like:

"Give me five different ways to describe an abandoned house in a horror story."

This helps keep your descriptions fresh and interesting without repeating the same tired phrases.

Another effective way to use ChatGPT is to have it **match the atmosphere to the protagonist's emotions.** Atmosphere in horror isn't static—it shifts with the character's state of mind. If your protagonist is panicked, the setting should feel chaotic and suffocating. If they're on edge, the setting should feel too quiet, too still, too unnatural.

You can prompt ChatGPT like this:

"Describe a hotel hallway from the point of view of a terrified person who feels like they're being followed."

The result will be language and imagery loaded with tension, reflecting your character's mindset.

You can even use ChatGPT to brainstorm **weather, lighting, and environmental conditions** that add to the atmosphere. Horror loves bad weather—storms, fog, oppressive heat. It also loves darkness, flickering lights, broken things. Ask:

"List five creepy weather conditions that could make a horror scene scarier."

You'll get ideas like heavy fog, constant distant thunder, a sudden power outage, oppressive heat that makes everything feel wrong.

And here's a little trick most writers don't think to use:

Ask ChatGPT to help you describe what the **characters can't see.** The empty space. The things half-seen in shadows. The absence of sound. Because in horror, it's often what's missing that makes the atmosphere terrifying.

For example, you can type:

"Describe the silence in a haunted house that makes it clear something is watching."

You'll get lines like: "The silence pressed against her ears like a weight, broken only by the sound of her own heartbeat—and something faint, almost a breath, hiding in the hush."

Once you start layering these descriptions in, your story will take on a life of its own. Readers won't just read about your haunted house—they'll feel like they're inside it, flinching at every sound, scanning every shadow.

But be careful not to overdo it. One of the biggest mistakes beginner horror writers make is drowning the story in description. Long paragraphs of atmospheric detail slow down the pacing and dull the scare factor. Atmosphere works best when it's used strategically, like seasoning. A few well-placed creepy details will stick in the reader's mind more than a page full of purple prose.

A great technique is to focus on the senses **your characters can't rely on.** If it's dark, lean into sound and touch. If it's noisy, lean into what they can see—or what they're trying to see. Sensory deprivation or overload heightens tension and fear.

You can also use ChatGPT to find fresh ways to describe common horror tropes. Instead of writing "The wind howled outside," ask:

"Give me three unsettling ways to describe the sound of wind in a horror scene."

You'll get creepier, more original options like, "The wind scraped against the window like fingernails" or "The air outside groaned like something trying to get in."

And don't forget that atmosphere isn't just about external description—it's about how the setting affects the characters internally. Use ChatGPT to help you describe the protagonist's reactions to the atmosphere. Their heart racing. Their skin prickling. The rising panic in their throat.

Finally, atmosphere isn't static. It should build, shift, and tighten around the reader like a noose. Start subtle—unsettling details, something slightly off—and escalate as the story progresses. The setting should grow darker, heavier, more claustrophobic as the horror ramps up.

Building Horror Themes That Linger

Anyone can write a scary scene. A sudden noise in the dark, a monster lunging from the shadows, a ghostly hand reaching out from nowhere—that's the easy part. But if you want your horror story to stick with readers long after they've finished it, you need something more than jump scares. You need a theme. A thread of meaning that runs beneath the terror. Something that creeps into the reader's mind after the book is closed and whispers, "That wasn't just a scary story—that was about something."

The best horror doesn't just scare. It makes people think, question, and shudder when they realize what the story was really about.

So how do you build horror themes that linger?

It starts with understanding what a theme is. A theme isn't your plot or your characters. It's the deeper idea your story is exploring. It's the fear beneath the fear. In horror, themes usually circle around things like loss, guilt, grief, isolation, identity, survival, or the darkness inside us all.

Think about some of the most iconic horror stories. *The Shining* isn't just about a haunted hotel—it's about addiction, abuse, and the slow unraveling of a family. *The Babadook* isn't just about a monster—it's about grief and mental illness. *Get Out* isn't just about body-snatching—it's about racism and the fear of losing autonomy.

When horror themes work, they leave a scar. They get under your skin because they're rooted in something real and human, not just supernatural terror.

So, the first step in building a strong horror theme is to ask yourself:

What is this story really about?

What fear are you trying to explore? What truth are you trying to reveal?

If you're stuck, this is where ChatGPT can help. Try typing:

"What are five deep, unsettling themes I can use in a horror story?"

You'll get options like:

- Fear of losing one's identity
- Fear of being powerless in the face of evil
- Fear of becoming what you hate
- Fear of being forgotten
- Fear of the past never staying buried

Pick the one that makes you uneasy—that's the one you should write.

Once you know your theme, it's time to weave it through every layer of your story.

Start with your **protagonist.** Their greatest fear, flaw, or trauma should tie directly into the theme. If your theme is about guilt, make sure your protagonist is running from something they did—or failed to do. If it's about isolation, make them someone who's already cut off from the world before the horror starts.

Next, look at your **villain or monster.** The best horror antagonists are physical manifestations of the story's theme. In *It Follows*, the creature represents sexual guilt and the fear of death. In *A Nightmare on Elm Street*, Freddy Krueger is the embodiment of generational trauma and buried secrets.

Ask yourself:

What would the physical version of my theme look like?

You can even use ChatGPT to help:

"Describe a horror monster that represents the fear of losing control."

You'll get creepy, specific ideas you can build into your story.

Then layer your theme into the **setting and atmosphere.** If your theme is about isolation, set your story somewhere remote. If it's about guilt, make the setting oppressive—crumbling walls, dark hallways, claustrophobic spaces. Every detail should serve the mood.

Your theme should also shape the **conflict and stakes.** What does your protagonist stand to lose beyond their life? Their sanity? Their loved ones? Their sense of self? Horror hits hardest when survival isn't the only thing on the line.

You can also use **symbols and motifs** to reinforce your theme. These can be subtle—recurring images, sounds, or objects that keep showing up. A broken mirror in every room. A child's lullaby playing when something terrible is about to happen. A red stain that keeps reappearing, no matter how much it's scrubbed away.

And don't forget the **ending.** A great horror theme doesn't just disappear when the monster is defeated. It lingers. Maybe the protagonist survives, but the real horror—the guilt, the grief, the trauma—remains. Maybe the villain wins, proving the theme true. Or maybe the protagonist changes, but not in the way they hoped. Horror themes work because they speak to the things we can't escape. They remind us that the real monsters are inside us, or around us, or waiting in the places we refuse to look.

One of the easiest ways to test if your theme is working is to ask yourself:

If I took out the monster, would this story still be scary?

If the answer is yes—if the underlying human fear is still there—you've built a theme that lingers.

You can even use ChatGPT to help tie it all together. Try:

"Summarize the theme of my horror story and suggest ways to make it clearer throughout the plot."

It'll help you connect the dots and make sure your theme is baked into every part of your story.

At the end of the day, the scares will grab your reader—but the theme is what will haunt them because once you've planted your theme, you need to drag your reader through it, one terrifying step at a time.

The Role of Backstory in Horror

Backstory is one of those things that can make or break a horror story. Too little, and your readers feel like the terror is happening in a vacuum. Too much, and you kill the tension by explaining everything away. The sweet spot is knowing how to use backstory to deepen the fear without slowing down the horror. When done right, backstory isn't an info dump—it's the shadow creeping behind your characters, the reason why the monster exists, the fuel behind the fear.

So let's talk about how to use backstory effectively in your horror narrative.

First, you need to understand **why backstory matters in horror.** Horror is about the unknown—but not about the meaningless. Readers want to understand why something terrible is happening, even if they never get the full picture. A good backstory gives weight to the horror. It answers the question: **Why is this happening to these characters, in this place, at this time?**

Think about iconic horror stories. In *The Ring*, there's the backstory of Samara, the cursed child whose death triggers the chain of terror. In *The Shining*, there's the bloody history of the Overlook Hotel, soaked into the walls and bleeding out over time. In *Hereditary*, the family's disturbing history of mental illness and occult connections is the thread that pulls the entire nightmare together.

The backstory in these stories isn't there to slow things down—it's there to make the present horror even scarier.

You can use ChatGPT to build this part fast and effectively. Type something like:

"Give me five disturbing backstories for a haunted house horror story."

You'll get options like:

- The house was built over a mass grave.
- The previous owners performed dark rituals in the basement.
- A family was murdered there, but the bodies were never found.
  You can then adapt, combine, or twist these ideas to fit your story.

When you're developing backstory, focus on three areas: **the location, the antagonist, and the protagonist.**

For the **location,** a creepy backstory makes the setting feel alive. Abandoned hospitals, cursed forests, forgotten towns—they all have a history. Let hints of that history seep into the story. Maybe the protagonist finds an old newspaper clipping. Maybe they hear stories from locals. Maybe the house itself shows scars of what happened—scratch marks on the walls, bloodstains that won't wash away.

You can use ChatGPT to generate these details, too:

"Describe three eerie historical events that could be tied to an abandoned hotel."

For the **antagonist,** a solid backstory gives them motive and depth. Your monster shouldn't just exist to kill or haunt—it should have a reason, even if that reason is tragic, twisted, or beyond human understanding. Was the villain betrayed? Cursed? Created by someone's mistake? Are they trying to get revenge, or are they trapped in a cycle they can't escape?

When the antagonist's backstory connects to the protagonist's journey, that's when the horror becomes personal and unforgettable.

For the **protagonist,** backstory gives emotional weight to the story. Maybe they've experienced trauma that makes them more vulnerable to the horror. Maybe they have a dark secret that ties them to the antagonist. Maybe the setting is tied to their childhood, an old place they swore they'd never return to.

You don't need to dump the protagonist's life story on the reader—but giving them a past that influences their actions makes them more real and their fear more believable.

One of the most effective ways to reveal backstory in horror is to **drip-feed it.** Don't stop the narrative to explain everything. Let the details emerge naturally, through clues, flashbacks, conversations, or unsettling discoveries. Make the reader piece it together like a puzzle—and when they do, it should make the present horror even worse.

For example, maybe your protagonist finds an old diary that hints at what happened in the house. Maybe the antagonist taunts them with knowledge of something from their past. Maybe they keep seeing the same image in their dreams, and only at the climax do they realize what it means.

You can use ChatGPT to help you structure this reveal. Try:

"Outline five ways to reveal a horror backstory gradually over a story."

You'll get ideas like using visions, scattered documents, unreliable witnesses, or even the environment itself.

Another thing to consider is **what to leave out.** Sometimes, the scariest stories don't explain everything. You can reveal just enough backstory to give the reader chills—but leave room for questions, for uncertainty. In *The Blair Witch Project,* we never see the witch, and the backstory is delivered in fragments. That mystery is what makes it so terrifying.

Symbolism is another powerful tool for backstory. Maybe the protagonist keeps seeing the same symbol carved into walls. Maybe the monster's appearance reflects something from the past. Use these subtle cues to hint at the backstory without spelling it all out.

Here's a practical method you can use when writing: Once you've planned your protagonist, antagonist, and setting, write a one-page "hidden history" of each. What's their dark secret? What's the horrible thing that happened before the story began? Then go back to your outline and look for places where you can drop hints about this history—without slowing down the action.

If you get stuck, ask ChatGPT:

"Help me write a chilling backstory for a horror story set in a remote cabin."

It will give you an instant, detailed history that you can fold into your narrative.

One final tip: Make sure your backstory isn't just interesting—it should tie directly into your theme. If your story is about guilt, make the backstory about a terrible mistake. If it's about isolation, make the past event something that cut the characters off from the world. That's how you make the horror feel inevitable, like the past was always coming back to claim them.

How to Make Death Matter in Your Story

In horror stories, people die. That's almost a rule of the genre. But here's the thing—death, by itself, isn't scary. It's common. It's expected. If you treat death like a throwaway event, it becomes background noise. Readers glaze over. Another victim. Another scream. Another body on the floor. What makes death powerful in horror is when it **means something**—when it has weight, consequence, and emotional punch.

Your job isn't to rack up a body count like a video game. Your job is to make every death land like a punch in the gut.

So how do you do that?

The first step is to make your characters feel real. This is something we've talked about throughout this book, but it bears repeating here. If the reader doesn't care about the character, they won't care when that character dies. You can't build tension around death unless the reader is invested in the person who's about to lose everything.

That doesn't mean every character needs a full backstory and emotional arc—but they need to feel like people. Give them quirks, relationships, hopes, fears. Show them laughing, arguing, dreaming. Then, when you kill them, it hurts.

A great technique is to make death **personal.** Death matters most when it affects your protagonist. Don't just kill random strangers. Kill the protagonist's friend, their partner, their sibling. Kill the person they've been trying to protect. Or worse—make the protagonist responsible for the death, directly or indirectly. That guilt will haunt them—and your reader—far longer than the death itself.

You can use ChatGPT to help build these connections fast. Type something like:

"Give me five ways to emotionally connect a horror protagonist to a character who will die later in the story."

You'll get answers like shared secrets, a promise made, a childhood friendship, or a fragile, tense relationship on the verge of healing.

Once you've built that connection, you can structure the death scene to maximize impact. **Don't rush it.** The actual moment of death can be fast, but the emotional weight should linger. Let the protagonist react. Let the reader feel the loss. And make sure the death changes something—it should escalate the stakes, shift the protagonist's arc, or reveal something terrifying about the antagonist.

Another important thing to consider is **how the character dies.** In horror, the method of death isn't just about gore or spectacle—it's about theme and emotion. A character who dies violently, screaming and alone, sends a very different message than a character who sacrifices themselves to save others. Think about what you want the death to mean.

And don't be afraid to make death messy. In horror stories, death isn't clean. It's ugly, unfair, terrifying. Lean into that. Make the reader squirm. Make them feel the panic, the fear, the weight of it. That's what makes death matter.

One of the best ways to make death hit hard is to tie it to the story's **theme.** If your story is about guilt, make the protagonist unable to save someone they love. If it's about isolation, make the protagonist watch someone die because they refused to trust anyone. If it's about fate, make every death feel inevitable, like the characters never had a chance.

You can use ChatGPT to brainstorm this connection. Try:

"Suggest five ways to tie a character's death to the theme of grief in a horror story."

You'll get ideas you can weave into your plot.

Another powerful technique is to use death to **advance the plot.** Don't kill characters randomly. Each death should change something. It should force the protagonist to act, reveal something new about the villain, or close off an escape route. Death should push the story forward, not stop it.

And here's a pro tip: **Build suspense around death.** Don't make it obvious who's going to die next. Horror is at its best when readers don't know who's safe. You can even subvert expectations—set up one character as the obvious victim, then kill someone else. Or let a character survive longer than expected, only to die when the reader starts to hope they'll make it.

You can also play with how death affects the survivors. In horror stories, the aftermath of death is just as important as the death itself. Show how it breaks your protagonist. Show how it twists them, drives them, or haunts them. Sometimes the real horror isn't the monster—it's the empty space left behind by the people who are gone.

And finally, don't be afraid to make death **permanent.** Too many horror stories cheapen death with last-minute resurrections, dream sequences, or fake-outs. If you want death to matter, let it stick. Let it leave a scar on the story, the protagonist, and the reader.

If you want to supercharge this, you can use ChatGPT to write the death scene itself. Type:

"Write an emotionally devastating death scene for a horror story protagonist's best friend."

Then tweak and refine until it's sharp enough to cut your reader's heart out.

Character Arcs in Horror: Who Lives, Who Dies

In horror stories, you know from the start that not everyone is going to make it. That's the promise of the genre. But what makes a horror story satisfying isn't just who dies or who survives—it's how the characters change over the course of the nightmare. It's about their **arc.** Horror is, at its core, about transformation. The characters who live, the ones who die, and the ones who lose everything but their lives all walk away changed—or they don't walk away at all.

So let's break down how to craft character arcs in horror and, just as importantly, how to decide who makes it to the end.

First off, every good horror story needs at least one character with a clear, compelling arc. Usually, this is your protagonist—the person whose journey we're following. Their arc doesn't have to be heroic or redemptive, but it should be dramatic. They should start in one place and end somewhere very different. Maybe they go from weak to strong, from skeptic to believer, from selfish to selfless, or from sane to shattered.

Horror is brutal, and that brutality changes people. That's why character arcs in horror are so powerful—they show how people break, adapt, or overcome in the face of terror.

A common structure in horror is the **Final Girl trope**—the lone survivor who outlasts the killer, the curse, or the monster. But what makes a Final Girl (or Final Boy, or Final Anyone) interesting isn't that they survive—it's what they've had to become to survive. Think about Laurie Strode in *Halloween* or Sidney Prescott in *Scream.* They start out as regular people. By the end, they're hardened, scarred, and forever changed.

When you're designing your character arcs, ask yourself:

What does this character fear the most?

What part of them needs to change to survive?

What will they lose along the way—friends, family, sanity, innocence?

What's the cost of survival?

You can even use ChatGPT to brainstorm these arcs fast. Try:

"Give me five possible character arcs for a horror protagonist who's afraid of being alone."

You'll get ideas like:

- They learn to rely on others, only to watch them die.
- They embrace solitude and become a cold survivor.
- They discover that the real horror isn't being alone—it's who they are when no one's watching.

Once you've mapped out your protagonist's arc, you need to think about your **supporting characters.** In horror, supporting characters aren't just cannon fodder—they serve a purpose. Each one should either highlight a different aspect of the protagonist's fear, contribute to the theme, or offer an emotional connection that raises the stakes.

Some supporting characters exist to die. That's fine—it's horror, after all. But don't treat them like redshirts. Give them personalities, relationships, flaws. Make the reader care, even a little, before you kill them. The death of a well-drawn character means something. It shocks, hurts, or motivates the protagonist. It raises the emotional cost of the story.

You can also design arcs for these characters, even if they're short. Maybe the tough, cynical character finally shows vulnerability right before they die. Maybe the selfish character sacrifices themselves at the last second. These small arcs add depth and make the deaths more impactful.

And here's a little trick: **Foreshadow who will live and who will die—but mislead your reader.** Set up the obvious survivor and kill them early. Let the quiet, background character make it to the end. Horror thrives on unpredictability, and flipping the reader's expectations keeps them on edge.

You can use ChatGPT to help plan this too. Type:

"List five ways to foreshadow a horror character's survival or death without being obvious."

Another thing to think about is the balance between death and survival. A horror story where everyone dies can feel hopeless. A story where everyone lives doesn't feel like horror at all. The sweet spot is somewhere in the middle. Enough death to feel dangerous, enough survival to offer a sliver of hope—or a twist of irony.

And remember, survival isn't always a happy ending. Sometimes the characters who live pay a higher price than the ones who die. They're left haunted, broken, fundamentally changed. That's the true horror.

If you want to go even deeper, you can structure your entire plot around how each character's arc ends. Who dies early to set the tone. Who lasts longer to raise the stakes. Who survives, and at what cost.

You can even map it out visually—draw a line for each major character and mark where they live, where they die, and how their arc evolves. If you're in a rush (and since you're writing this in one day, you probably are), you can ask ChatGPT to help:

"Create a character arc chart for a horror story with five main characters, showing who lives and who dies."

Finally, tie each arc back to your theme. If your story is about guilt, make the survivor someone who's forced to live with their mistakes. If it's about isolation, maybe the survivor is the one who pushed everyone away and now has no one left. If it's about fate, make the deaths feel inevitable—like no one ever had a chance.

When you do this right, your readers won't just be scared by who dies. They'll be haunted by why they died, what it meant, and how it changed the people who survived.

The Power of the Unseen: Implied Horror

If there's one thing that separates a good horror story from a great one, it's knowing when **not** to show the monster. Some of the scariest horror stories ever written, filmed, or told rely on a single, powerful technique—**implied horror.** The power of the unseen, the unsaid, the unknown. What your reader imagines is almost always more terrifying than anything you can describe.

Horror is a psychological game, and implied horror plays directly into how the human brain works. We fear the unknown. We fear what we can't see, can't explain, can't control. When you show the monster in full, that fear starts to shrink. But when you leave things in the shadows, when you suggest something terrible without spelling it out, the reader's mind goes wild filling in the blanks.

That's what implied horror does—it forces the reader to become part of the horror.

Let's break down how you can use this technique in your story.

First, understand that implied horror is all about **suggestion, not explanation.** Instead of describing the monster's sharp teeth and dripping claws, describe the scratch marks on the door. Describe the protagonist waking up with dirt under their fingernails and no memory of how it got there. Describe the smell of something rotten drifting through the house with no source.

It's about what's **missing.** The empty chair that's suddenly rocking. The child's laughter echoing through an abandoned hospital. The bloody handprint on the wall with no footprints leading to or away from it.

You can use ChatGPT to help brainstorm these eerie, subtle details. Try:

"Give me ten examples of implied horror moments in a haunted house story."

You'll get ideas like:

- The TV turns on by itself, but plays static with a faint whisper underneath.
- The protagonist keeps waking up to find muddy footprints circling their bed.
- A family photo on the wall changes subtly each day—people disappearing from it one by one.

Another way to use implied horror is to manipulate **sound and silence.** In your descriptions, focus on what the characters hear—or don't hear. A knock at the door with no one there. A voice calling from another room when the house is empty. The absence of familiar sounds, like birdsong or traffic, that suddenly makes the world feel wrong.

You can even ask ChatGPT to help you craft these moments. Type:

"Describe a creepy, unsettling silence in a horror story."

The reply might give you something like:

"The silence pressed against her ears like a living thing, broken only by her own breathing—and something faint, like a breath not her own, curling beneath the quiet."

Another important tool in implied horror is **character reaction.** Sometimes, what's scary isn't the thing itself—it's how the characters react to it. Show their growing paranoia. Their jumpiness. Their inability to explain what's happening. Let the reader feel their unease through body language, fragmented thoughts, hesitant dialogue.

Restraint is key. Don't over-explain. Don't answer every question. Horror thrives on mystery, and implied horror is the art of leaving enough room for the reader's imagination to run wild. When you lay out everything too neatly—what the monster looks like, what its rules are, what it wants—you kill the fear.

Think about stories like *The Blair Witch Project.* You never see the witch. You never get clear answers. And that's why it terrified audiences. The horror was in what you couldn't see, in the sounds at night, in the increasingly frantic reactions of the characters.

Or *A Quiet Place.* For much of the movie, the monsters are implied through sound and movement. It's the tension of what's coming, not the monster itself, that drives the fear.

Implied horror also works well when tied to your story's **theme.** If your horror story is about grief, maybe the implied horror is the sense that something or someone is still lingering. If it's about guilt, maybe the protagonist keeps seeing signs of the person they wronged, but can't prove it.

You can use ChatGPT to help brainstorm these connections. Try:

"List five ways to use implied horror to support a theme of guilt in a horror story."

You'll get suggestions like:

- The protagonist keeps hearing the dead person's voice in static.
- Their reflection moves a second too late.
- They find messages written in their own handwriting with no memory of writing them.

A good rule of thumb is: **The more you explain, the safer the reader feels.** When you pull back the curtain and reveal the monster, the reader's imagination shuts down. But when you leave things unsaid, their mind keeps turning, keeps wondering, keeps fearing.

That doesn't mean you can never show the horror. Sometimes you need to let the monster off the leash. But the longer you can delay that moment—the more you can suggest, imply, and hint—the stronger the payoff will be when it finally happens.

And sometimes, the best payoff is to never show it at all.

Another technique is to let the reader wonder if the horror is even real. Implied horror blurs the line between reality and imagination. Is the protagonist losing their mind? Is there something supernatural happening, or is it all in their head? That uncertainty is where real fear lives.

You can structure entire stories around this ambiguity. The protagonist finds signs, hears sounds, sees things out of the corner of their eye—but can never prove anything. The horror builds because neither they nor the reader can tell what's real.

Playing with Point of View for Maximum Terror

If there's one tool in your horror-writing toolbox that can change everything about how scary your story feels, it's **point of view.** The perspective you choose isn't just about style—it's about how close the reader gets to the fear, how much information they have, and how trapped they feel inside the nightmare you're building.

Point of view is the lens through which your reader experiences the horror. Choose wisely, and you can crank the tension to unbearable levels.

Let's break down how you can use point of view (POV) to make your horror story scarier, more claustrophobic, more personal—and how you can use ChatGPT to help you sharpen it.

First, the three most common POVs:

First Person ("I")

This is the most intimate, most claustrophobic choice. When you write in first person, you're locking the reader inside the protagonist's head. They see what the protagonist sees. They feel what the protagonist feels. And in horror, that's incredibly powerful.

Why? Because the reader can't step back. They can't pull away. They're stuck in the protagonist's terror, their panic, their confusion. They don't get the luxury of knowing what's really going on—they only know what the protagonist knows, and that limited knowledge ramps up the tension.

But there's a catch. First person horror often means your protagonist has to survive—because they're telling the story. You can still have devastating losses, shocking twists, and unreliable narration (which is fantastic in horror), but the reader knows they'll at least make it to the final page.

You can use ChatGPT to help craft a strong first-person voice. Try:

"Write a paragraph in a terrified first-person voice about being trapped in a haunted house."

You'll get a visceral, immediate draft you can refine and personalize.

Close Third Person ("He/She/They")

Close third person works almost like first person, but with a little more breathing room. You stay inside the protagonist's head, but with a touch of distance. This gives you more flexibility in language and allows you to pull away from the protagonist when needed—but you can still create that tight, tense experience.

This is a great choice if you want to follow one main character but still describe things they wouldn't notice—like how the shadows shift behind them or how the antagonist is closing in. You can also create dramatic irony by letting the reader know something the protagonist doesn't.

Omniscient Third Person

This is the widest POV—you can jump into any character's head, zoom out, give the reader information no one in the story has. In horror, omniscient POV can work, but it's trickier. The more you explain, the more you pull the reader out of the fear. Horror thrives on **limitation**—what the reader doesn't know is often scarier than what they do.

That said, you can use omniscient POV to show how widespread or inevitable the horror is. Think of stories where the whole town is doomed, or where evil is creeping toward everyone, not just one protagonist.

You can ask ChatGPT to help you test different POVs. For example:

"Write the same scary scene in first person, close third person, and omniscient third person."

Reading them side by side will help you decide which one hits hardest.

Now, beyond these traditional POVs, you can get creative and experimental—because horror rewards playing with structure.

Unreliable Narrators

One of the best ways to weaponize POV is to make your narrator unreliable. When the reader can't trust the protagonist, everything becomes unsettling. Are the ghosts real? Is the protagonist hallucinating? Are they lying to us—or themselves? That uncertainty keeps readers off balance.

Think of *The Yellow Wallpaper*, *The Tell-Tale Heart*, or *House of Leaves*. The horror isn't just in what's happening—it's in the fact that you can't trust who's telling you about it.

You can use ChatGPT to help brainstorm unreliable narrator tricks. Try:

"List five ways to show an unreliable narrator in a horror story."

Second Person ("You")

This is a rarer choice, but when used well, it's incredibly creepy. Second person makes the reader the protagonist. Suddenly, **they're** the one walking down the dark hallway, hearing the floorboards creak, realizing they're not alone.

Used sparingly, second person POV can make horror uncomfortably intimate. It's like the story is speaking directly to the reader, dragging them into the nightmare.

If you want to experiment, ask ChatGPT:

"Write a creepy horror scene in second person POV."

You'll get a chilling, direct scene that feels like it's happening to the reader.

Multiple POVs

Another option is to tell your story from multiple points of view. Maybe you follow the protagonist, the antagonist, and a few victims. This can widen the scope of your horror and create dramatic irony—letting the reader see the monster creeping up on a character who has no idea.

But be careful. Too many POV shifts can dilute the fear. The more heads the reader jumps between, the less intimate the story feels. If you use this approach, make sure each POV is distinct and meaningful.

Found Footage / Epistolary POV

Horror also loves stories told through journals, letters, news articles, or "found footage." This creates a layer of distance and mystery—the reader isn't getting the story firsthand, but piecing it together from fragments. That structure can be terrifying because it feels real, like you're reading something you weren't supposed to find.

You can use ChatGPT to help structure these elements. Try:

"Create a series of journal entries that tell a horror story about a cursed cabin."

At the end of the day, POV is about **control.** You're deciding how much the reader knows, how close they get to the fear, how much distance or intimacy they feel. In horror, less is often more. The narrower the perspective, the scarier the experience.

So when you sit down to write, ask yourself:

Whose nightmare is this?

How close do I want the reader to get?

What will they see—and what will they miss?

In the next chapter, we're going to talk about how to pace all of this—the reveals, the scares, the character arcs—so that every piece falls into place and keeps the reader breathless until the final, terrifying page.

How to Pace a Horror Story So It Builds to a Climax

Pacing is everything in horror. You can have the creepiest villain, the darkest setting, and the most bone-chilling scares—but if you dump all your horror too soon or drag it out too long, your story will fall flat. A horror story is like winding a jack-in-the-box; the tension builds slowly, click by click, until it finally explodes. Your job is to control how fast you turn that crank.

In this chapter, we're going to talk about how to pace your horror story so it keeps the reader hooked, tightens the tension scene by scene, and delivers a knockout climax that leaves them breathless.

First, let's talk about **why pacing matters in horror.** Horror isn't like action, where everything explodes from the first page. Horror is about tension. It's about anticipation. Fear isn't just about what happens—it's about what might happen. A well-paced horror story makes the reader dread turning the page, but unable to stop.

Good horror pacing works like a wave. You build tension, release it just a little, then build it higher. Over and over, until you hit the peak at the climax. Think of it like tightening a noose. The more you pull, the less room the reader has to breathe.

So how do you actually structure that?

Start with a **slow burn.** Horror stories usually begin with normalcy—a world that feels familiar, safe, or even boring. This is important because the reader needs something to lose. If the story starts at full chaos, there's nowhere to go. Give them a false sense of security. Let them get to know the characters. Show the setting in daylight, when everything seems fine.

But even in these early scenes, you want to plant seeds of unease. Small, subtle things that tell the reader something isn't right. A strange noise. A fleeting shadow. An uncomfortable conversation. These are your first hints of dread.

You can use ChatGPT to help brainstorm these early tension-builders. Try:

"List five subtle, creepy details to plant in the first chapter of a horror story."

You'll get atmospheric, unsettling touches you can use to start winding the tension without tipping your hand.

Next, you want to start **escalating the tension.** Each scene should tighten the screws. The strange things get stranger. The protagonist's fears grow. The danger becomes clearer—but never all at once. You want to drip-feed information. Give the reader just enough to keep them guessing, but hold back the full picture.

A great technique here is to use **peaks and valleys.** Don't keep everything at a constant high tension—readers will get numb. After a scary scene, give the reader (and your protagonist) a moment to breathe. A quiet scene. A false sense of relief. Then hit them harder with the next scare.

This rise and fall keeps the tension fresh and exhausting—in the best possible way.

The middle of your story is where you want to **raise the stakes.** The protagonist should be in deeper danger. They should start realizing what they're up against. Maybe a friend dies. Maybe they find evidence of something horrifying. Maybe they start to lose their grip on reality.

This is also where you can start tightening the plot threads. The little clues you planted early on start to come together. The backstory gets revealed piece by piece. The theme starts to shine through.

If you're stuck, you can use ChatGPT to help structure this. Try:

"Outline five key events in the middle of a horror story that escalate tension."

Now, as you approach the final third of your story, you want to build toward the **climax.** This is where the pacing shifts from slow-burn to full-throttle. Your protagonist should be cornered, desperate, out of options. The reader should feel like the walls are closing in, the clock is ticking, and there's no way out.

Everything should converge here—backstory, character arcs, scares, reveals. The monster is loose. The secrets are out. The protagonist is facing their worst fear.

But here's the trick: **Don't let the climax drag.** After all that slow build-up, your climax should hit fast and hard. It should be messy, chaotic, terrifying. Readers shouldn't have time to breathe.

A lot of beginner writers make the mistake of over-explaining in the climax. Don't do that. This is where the story should move at breakneck speed. Your protagonist is fighting, running, confronting the horror. If there are big twists or revelations, drop them quickly and keep moving.

Once you've hit the climax—whether the protagonist survives, escapes, defeats the monster, or dies—you need to give the reader a moment of **release.** Horror stories often have short, quiet resolutions. A chapter, a few pages, even just a paragraph. Enough to let the reader process what happened and feel the lingering dread.

You can also use the ending to tie your theme together. Maybe the protagonist survived but is traumatized. Maybe the monster is gone, but something worse has been unleashed. Maybe the story ends with a question that will haunt the reader long after they finish.

ChatGPT can help you structure this entire pacing arc quickly. Try:

"Outline the pacing of a horror story in five acts, focusing on tension build-up and climax."

You'll get a blueprint you can follow to keep your story tight, scary, and satisfying.

And one final tip: **Trust your reader.** Horror pacing isn't about overwhelming them with information or scares. It's about giving them just enough to feel the noose tightening around their neck, page by terrifying page.

Using ChatGPT to Generate Creepy Supporting Characters

Every horror story needs more than just a protagonist and a monster. It needs a full cast of people who populate the world—friends, neighbors, victims, red herrings, and weirdos who hover on the edge of the plot. These supporting characters don't just fill space; they add flavor, tension, misdirection, and sometimes, an extra layer of horror.

And the best part? You don't have to rack your brain for hours trying to dream up these characters. You've got ChatGPT in your corner, and when you know how to use it, you can populate your horror world with creepy, unsettling, unforgettable supporting characters in minutes.

First, let's talk about **why supporting characters matter in horror.** These characters serve multiple purposes. They can make the protagonist's world feel real and lived-in. They can raise the stakes by dying, disappearing, or turning on the protagonist. They can provide exposition, serve as obstacles, or offer false hope. And sometimes, they're scarier than the monster.

Think about how often the creepiest character in a horror story isn't the villain—it's the person who seems normal but says something just a little too strange. The neighbor who watches from the window. The child who hums an old, forgotten song. The friend who starts acting distant and cold.

These characters stick in the reader's mind because they feel like something is wrong, even if they can't put their finger on it.

So how do you use ChatGPT to create them?

It starts with a simple prompt. Try:

"Give me ten unsettling supporting character ideas for a psychological horror story."

You'll get back a list of characters like:

- A friendly old woman who always knows too much about the protagonist's nightmares.
- A young child who draws disturbing pictures of things that haven't happened yet.
- A priest who refuses to talk about the town's history but carries a knife everywhere.
- A neighbor who's always watching from his upstairs window but never leaves the house.
- A best friend who seems helpful but slowly starts gaslighting the protagonist.

Once you've got a few ideas, start thinking about how they fit into your story. Supporting characters in horror work best when they serve one of three functions:

1. Tension Builder

These are the characters who make the protagonist (and reader) uneasy without doing anything overtly villainous. They say the wrong thing at the wrong time. They know something they shouldn't. They disappear when things go bad.

You can use ChatGPT to help flesh out their dialogue. Try:

"Write a creepy conversation between a horror protagonist and an unsettling old man at a gas station."

You'll get eerie, ambiguous dialogue that ramps up the tension without giving too much away.

2. Victim or Sacrifice

Some supporting characters exist to die—or worse. But don't treat them like disposable meat. If you want your readers to care when someone dies, give that character personality. Maybe it's the protagonist's best friend. Maybe it's a local cop who tries to help. Maybe it's the one person who believed the protagonist when no one else did.

You can use ChatGPT to quickly sketch out their personality. Try:

"Describe a sympathetic character in a horror story who will die in the second act."

3. Red Herring or Misdirection

One of the best ways to keep readers on edge is to make them suspect the wrong person. Creepy supporting characters are perfect for this. The reclusive neighbor. The untrustworthy co-worker. The stranger who seems too helpful.

ChatGPT can help you brainstorm these misdirection characters. Ask:

"Give me five creepy supporting characters who might be mistaken for the villain."

Once you've created these characters, don't just drop them in and forget about them. Weave them into the fabric of your story. Let them interact with the protagonist in unsettling ways. Let the reader wonder: **Is this person part of the horror, or just another victim?**

You can also use supporting characters to reflect your story's **theme.** If your theme is about isolation, make sure the protagonist is surrounded by people who ignore them, dismiss them, or leave them behind. If it's about guilt, maybe one of the supporting characters knows the protagonist's secret and keeps hinting at it.

And don't forget: the way your supporting characters **react** to the horror can raise the stakes. Maybe they try to help but fail. Maybe they betray the protagonist when things get bad. Maybe they become possessed, corrupted, or reveal they were part of the horror all along.

If you want to make things even easier, you can ask ChatGPT to help you map these characters into your plot. Try:

"Create a supporting character list for a horror story, including their relationship to the protagonist, personality, and role in the plot."

You'll get a ready-made cast you can drop right into your outline.

Another useful exercise is to generate **background quirks** that make your supporting characters memorable. Tiny details that make them feel real and creepy.

You can type:

"Give me ten eerie habits or quirks for horror supporting characters."

You'll get gems like:

- Always humming the same lullaby.
- Collecting broken dolls and leaving them around town.

- Asking personal questions they shouldn't know the answers to.
- Wearing the same outfit every day, no matter the weather.
- Scratching the same spot on their arm until it bleeds.

These quirks can make even minor characters unsettling and memorable.

Finally, when writing your scenes, use your supporting characters to **shift the mood.** A seemingly harmless interaction can turn dark fast. A casual conversation can reveal something terrifying. A friendly neighbor can suddenly be at the window in the middle of the night.

The reader never knows who to trust. That's what makes horror work.

In the next chapter, we're going to shift from characters to setting—specifically, how to build **believable and terrifying horror worlds** that feel alive and dangerous.

Because now that you've got your cast, you need to give them a nightmare to live in.

World-Building in Horror without Slowing the Pace

When most writers think about world-building, they picture sprawling fantasy worlds, maps of kingdoms, and pages of lore. But world-building isn't just for epic fantasy—it's just as important in horror. The difference is, in horror, you don't have the luxury of slowing things down to explain your world. Horror relies on pacing, tension, and a creeping sense of dread. So your challenge is to build a believable, immersive horror world **without slowing the story to a crawl.**

Let's break down how to do that and how ChatGPT can help you nail it.

First, understand what **world-building** means in horror. It's not about building an entire universe—it's about creating a setting, mood, and logic that feels real enough for the horror to hit hard. It's the rules of your world. The history of the cursed town. The legend of the monster. The way the darkness creeps into every corner of the protagonist's life.

You don't need pages of exposition. You just need to make the world feel solid and alive—so when things go wrong, the reader believes it.

The trick is to do it **on the fly.** You build your horror world as the story moves, planting little details and hints without stopping the action.

For example, instead of writing a long paragraph explaining that the town has a history of mysterious disappearances, you can have a character casually mention it:

"You know, people have been vanishing around here for years. My uncle always said this place was cursed."

That one line does more world-building than a full-page history lesson—and it keeps the tension moving.

You can use ChatGPT to help you drop these world-building details in naturally. Try:

"Write three creepy local legends a bartender might mention in a horror story."

You'll get snippets you can sprinkle into dialogue or background scenes.

Another technique is to use **setting as world-building.** Let the details of the environment tell the reader something's wrong without spelling it out. Describe the peeling paint on the walls, the boarded-up houses, the cold, damp air that never quite lifts. Show how the townspeople avoid eye contact. Let the world feel haunted.

You can ask ChatGPT:

"Describe a small town with a dark, unsettling history without explaining it outright."

Objects are another great tool. A cracked photograph, a bloodstained letter, an old newspaper clipping—all of these can suggest a larger, darker world without slowing the pace. Your protagonist can stumble across them mid-scene, giving the reader a glimpse of the horror's roots while the story keeps moving.

Rules are another part of horror world-building. Every good horror story has rules, even if they're supernatural. The monster only comes out after midnight. The ghost can't enter holy ground. Breaking the rules gets you killed.

But here's the thing—you don't need to dump all the rules on the reader at once. Let the characters learn them the hard way. A friend dies because they broke the rule. The protagonist survives because they figure one out. This method keeps the tension high and the pace moving.

You can use ChatGPT to brainstorm these rules. Try:

"Give me five creepy rules for surviving a haunted forest."

You'll get original, unsettling ideas you can weave into your story as obstacles or revelations.

History and backstory are also part of world-building—but again, you need to reveal them strategically. Instead of writing a full chapter about the tragic history of your haunted house, drop breadcrumbs. A character finds an old journal. A neighbor tells a half-remembered story. Strange graffiti on a wall hints at something forgotten.

Each time you reveal a piece, it should push the story forward, raise the stakes, or deepen the mystery. If you're writing your horror story in one day, use ChatGPT to generate these background details quickly and insert them where they'll have the most impact.

Try:

"Write a short, creepy backstory for an abandoned mental hospital that will be revealed halfway through a horror story."

The key is to think of world-building in horror like **set dressing in a haunted house.** You don't need to explain every cobweb and creaking floorboard—you just need enough detail to make the reader feel trapped inside. The horror itself will do the rest.

Another way to layer in world-building without slowing the story is through **character behavior.** How do the locals act? What are they afraid of? What do they refuse to talk about? The way characters react to the world around them tells the reader everything they need to know.

For example, in a town cursed by a vengeful ghost, maybe the townspeople avoid certain streets after dark. Maybe they whisper prayers when they pass the old church. These little behaviors hint at a bigger, darker world without stopping the plot.

You can even use ChatGPT to generate these reactions. Ask:

"List five eerie ways a small town's residents might behave if they believe their town is cursed."

And don't forget—sometimes the **absence** of information builds the world better than an explanation. Leave things unsaid. Let the reader wonder why no one goes into the basement, why the forest is so quiet, why the town's records stop after a certain year.

The unknown is one of horror's greatest tools, and your world-building should lean into it.

One last tip: use your world-building to **mirror your protagonist's journey.** If your story is about isolation, make the world empty and cold. If it's about buried secrets, make the town's history full of missing pages and silent witnesses. Let the world reflect the horror inside your characters.

Horror Tropes You Can Use or Twist

Let's get one thing straight—**tropes aren't bad.** A lot of writers hear the word "trope" and immediately think it means cliché, something overdone, something to avoid. But the truth is, tropes are the building blocks of genre fiction. They're patterns, ideas, and devices that readers recognize and expect. In horror, tropes are like the creaking door in a haunted house—you know it's coming, but it still makes you jump if used well.

The real magic happens when you either **lean into a trope and do it well** or **twist it into something fresh and terrifying.** And with ChatGPT on your side, you can generate, reshape, and reinvent tropes faster than you can say "don't go in the basement."

Let's break down some of the most common horror tropes you can use—and how to twist them to make your story stand out.

1. The Final Girl

This is probably the most famous horror trope. The last survivor. The one who outsmarts the killer, fights back, or just gets lucky enough to live. We've seen it a hundred times—Laurie in *Halloween*, Sidney in *Scream*, countless others.

If you want to use this trope, make your Final Girl (or Final Boy, or Final Anyone) interesting. Give them flaws, secrets, something personal at stake beyond survival.

Or twist it. Maybe the Final Girl doesn't survive. Maybe she becomes the monster. Maybe she was the villain all along.

You can use ChatGPT to help flip this trope:

"Suggest three ways to subvert the Final Girl trope in a horror story."

2. The Isolated Setting

A cabin in the woods. An abandoned hospital. A snowed-in hotel. Isolation is a classic horror trope because it removes help and traps the characters.

You can absolutely use this, but look for fresh spins. Maybe the isolation isn't physical—it's emotional. Maybe the protagonist is surrounded by people but utterly alone. Or flip the setting entirely—set your horror story in a crowded city where isolation comes from being invisible.

3. The Sinister Child

Creepy kids are a horror staple. Think *The Omen*, *The Ring*, or *Children of the Corn*. There's something inherently unsettling about innocence corrupted.

You can use this trope straight, or you can twist it. Maybe the child isn't evil—they're being used by something else. Or maybe the adults are the real monsters, and the child is the only one who sees the truth.

4. The Forbidden Place

Another go-to trope: the place everyone knows you shouldn't go, but someone always does. The haunted house. The cursed town. The old asylum.

You can lean into this and make the place itself a character. Or you can twist it—maybe the forbidden place is safe, and the real danger is outside. Maybe the protagonist is the one who cursed it.

5. The Unheeded Warning

Someone always warns the protagonist not to do something, and they ignore it. Classic setup for horror.

The twist? Maybe the warning is wrong. Maybe the person giving the warning is the villain. Or maybe the protagonist listens—and that's when everything really goes wrong.

6. The Monster You Can't See

This is implied horror 101. The thing in the shadows. The thing you only glimpse. Think *The Blair Witch Project* or *It Follows.*

If you use this, build tension by never fully showing the monster. Or, twist it—what if the monster is only invisible to the protagonist? Everyone else can see it, but no one will tell them why.

7. The Cursed Object

The videotape, the mirror, the artifact that brings doom. A simple but effective trope.

The twist? Maybe the curse is a lie. Maybe the object isn't cursed—it's protective, and breaking it releases the real horror.

8. Everyone Dies

The bleak, nihilistic horror ending where no one makes it out alive.

You can absolutely go this route—but know that it's hard to pull off without depressing the reader. The twist? Maybe someone survives, but at a terrible cost. Or the monster dies, but something worse is unleashed.

9. The Creepy Local

The gas station attendant who warns you. The old neighbor who knows the dark history. The friendly cop who's a little too interested.

This trope is great for world-building, but you can twist it. Maybe the creepy local is the only sane person. Maybe they're trying to save the protagonist, but no one listens.

10. The Haunted Protagonist

Not just by ghosts—but by guilt, grief, trauma. Their personal demons fuel the real horror.

You should absolutely use this trope because it ties the horror to character. The twist? Maybe the horror is entirely internal. Maybe there's no monster—just the protagonist's unraveling mind.

How to Use ChatGPT to Weaponize Tropes

One of the fastest ways to come up with fresh, terrifying tropes is to get ChatGPT involved. You can use prompts like:

"List ten overused horror tropes I can twist in my story."

"Suggest five unique ways to flip common horror tropes."

"Generate three new horror tropes based on modern fears."

You'll get lists, ideas, and even full scene concepts you can drop straight into your outline.

The goal isn't to avoid tropes—it's to use them smartly. Readers love the familiar beats of horror, but they also love being surprised when those beats go sideways.

The Hero's Journey in Horror Stories

When people think about the Hero's Journey, they usually picture epic fantasy tales or big-screen superhero stories. But the truth is, horror stories use the Hero's Journey just as much—and sometimes even more effectively—because horror is, at its heart, a journey of survival, transformation, and facing the darkness, both outside and within.

If you want your horror story to hit hard, to have that extra layer beneath the screams and jump scares, you should absolutely build it around a Hero's Journey. And the best part? You can use ChatGPT to help structure this journey fast so you can write your horror story in one day without getting lost.

So let's walk through how the Hero's Journey works in horror and how to apply it.

The Ordinary World

This is where your protagonist starts—before the nightmare begins. In a horror story, this world usually feels mundane, familiar, even boring. The small town. The quiet neighborhood. The group of friends on a weekend trip. But you should sprinkle in unease right away—a bad dream, a strange news story, a feeling that something's off.

This is where you establish who the protagonist is and what their biggest fear or flaw is, because that's what the horror will target.

The Call to Adventure

In horror, the "call" is the first hint that something's wrong. A mysterious phone call. A strange noise in the basement. A loved one goes missing. The protagonist could ignore it—but they don't. Whether out of curiosity, duty, or circumstance, they step toward the darkness.

Refusal of the Call

This is a staple of horror. The protagonist denies what's happening. They rationalize it. They tell themselves there's no such thing as ghosts, or that the serial killer isn't after them. This denial creates tension and frustration, because the reader already knows: something is coming.

Meeting the Mentor

In horror, the "mentor" is often someone who knows what's really going on. The creepy old woman who warns them. The local historian who knows the town's dark secrets. Sometimes the mentor is unreliable, unhelpful, or already dead. But they leave behind a clue, a rule, or a warning.

You can use ChatGPT to generate these characters quickly. Try:

"Create five creepy mentor characters for a horror story."

Crossing the Threshold

This is the point of no return. In horror, this is when the protagonist enters the haunted house, moves to the cursed town, plays with the Ouija board, or uncovers the terrible truth. From here on, they can't go back to the ordinary world.

Tests, Allies, and Enemies

Now the horror escalates. The protagonist faces small, terrifying encounters. They meet allies—friends, family, people who may or may not survive. They encounter enemies—sometimes obvious, sometimes hidden. The monster starts hunting them. The body count rises. The protagonist is tested, over and over.

This is where you let your pacing tighten, your scares escalate, and your protagonist start to crack.

Approach to the Inmost Cave

This is when the protagonist finally understands the real danger. It's not just a haunted house—it's something personal. The monster knows their deepest fear. The ghosts aren't random—they're tied to something the protagonist did or failed to do.

The "Inmost Cave" in horror is often literal—a basement, an attic, an underground lair—but it's also emotional. It's the place where the protagonist has to confront their own demons.

The Ordeal

This is your horror story's climax. Everything falls apart. People die. Secrets are revealed. The protagonist faces the monster, the villain, or the source of the horror—and almost dies in the process.

The Ordeal is brutal. It's messy. It's terrifying. And it should push the protagonist to their absolute limit.

Reward (Seizing the Sword)

In fantasy, this is when the hero gets the treasure. In horror, it's rarely that clean. The "reward" might be survival. It might be a weapon, a key, or a final piece of knowledge that can end the nightmare. Sometimes it's just the realization of what's really happening.

The Road Back

In horror, the road back isn't safe. Just because the monster is dead doesn't mean the horror is over. The protagonist might still be hunted. They might be bleeding, broken, running for their life.

This is where you can squeeze in one last scare—the classic "hand reaching from the grave" moment.

Resurrection

This is the true climax. The protagonist faces one final test. In horror, this is often the moment they become something else. They're no longer the person they were at the start. They're hardened, scarred, stronger—or destroyed.

Maybe they defeat the monster. Maybe they sacrifice themselves. Maybe they realize they were the monster all along.

Return with the Elixir

In horror, there's rarely a happy ending. But there is a return. The protagonist may survive, but they're changed forever. Sometimes the "elixir" is knowledge—what not to do next time. Sometimes it's loss. Sometimes it's the haunting truth that the horror never really ends.

You can use ChatGPT to map out this entire structure in minutes. Try:

"Outline a horror story using the Hero's Journey structure."

You'll get a detailed breakdown you can use to write quickly and efficiently.

The beauty of using the Hero's Journey in horror is that it gives your story structure and emotional weight. Readers won't just be scared—they'll be invested in the protagonist's transformation.

Turning Ordinary Places into Nightmares

One of the coolest tricks in horror storytelling isn't building creepy castles or cursed woods. It's taking a place your readers know—a house, a school, a hospital, a grocery store—and making it terrifying. There's something way scarier about familiar spaces turned sinister because it tells the reader, "You're not safe anywhere."

You don't need graveyards and foggy forests to scare people. Sometimes, the scariest thing is when your own home becomes the place you can't escape from.

So how do you turn ordinary places into nightmares?

It starts with **details.** Horror lives in the cracks, the forgotten corners, the things you don't notice until something's wrong. You want the reader to feel like they're in a normal place—but slowly realize it's changing. Or worse, realize it's always been wrong, but they never saw it before.

Let's start with a basic place: a house. Everyone knows what a house looks like. So how do you make it scary?

You don't need to tell the reader it's haunted right away. Instead, focus on sensory details that feel slightly off. The silence that's too quiet. The shadows that seem too dark. The air that feels heavy when you step inside.

You can ask ChatGPT to help you find these details. Try:

"Describe an ordinary living room in a creepy, unsettling way."

You'll get things like:

The TV screen flickering even though it's unplugged. A faint smell of something burning with no source. Family photos where the faces seem to change every time you look.

Those tiny details turn a normal place into a nightmare.

Another way to make ordinary places scary is to use **unfamiliar angles.** Take something your readers know and describe it from a perspective they never think about. The flicker of a streetlight reflected in a puddle. The way a hallway looks when you're crawling on the floor, hiding from something. The sound of footsteps upstairs when you live alone.

Isolation is another key. Take a place that should be full of life—a school, a hospital, a grocery store—and make it empty. People gone, lights flickering, something breathing in the darkness. Readers know what these places feel like when they're normal, so when you strip away the safety, it's terrifying.

ChatGPT can help you brainstorm these settings fast. Try:

"List five ordinary places that could be terrifying when empty."

You'll get options like:

- An elementary school at night.
- A shopping mall after hours.
- A subway station with no trains running.
- A hospital wing closed off for renovations.

- A motel off the highway with no other cars in the lot.

But you can also make an ordinary place scary **without emptying it.** Sometimes, the people are what make it terrifying. A diner where everyone turns to look at you when you walk in—and doesn't stop staring. A neighborhood where the residents smile too much, wave too much, watch you too closely. That feeling that something is just not right.

You can use ChatGPT to help develop these moments. Ask:

"Write a creepy scene set in an ordinary coffee shop."

You'll get a scene where the normal becomes unnerving fast.

Another technique is to weaponize **routine.** Horror loves repetition that feels wrong. The same song playing every time the protagonist enters a store. A neighbor who mows the lawn at midnight. The protagonist's alarm clock going off at exactly 3:13 AM every night, even when it's unplugged.

These little cracks in normalcy build dread without needing gore or monsters.

And don't forget the power of **liminal spaces.** These are places that exist in transition—hallways, stairwells, waiting rooms, empty parking lots at night. Liminal spaces already feel a little eerie because they're not meant to be places where you stay. They're designed to pass through. So when something terrifying happens there, it hits harder.

If you want, you can ask ChatGPT:

"Describe a liminal space in an unsettling way for a horror story."

You'll get creepy, atmospheric text you can drop right into your scenes.

You can also turn ordinary places into nightmares by playing with **time.** The office building at noon feels safe. That same building at 3 AM, echoing and empty, is something else entirely. Describe how the place changes at night—the way the lights flicker, the shadows stretch, the sounds echo too much.

Memory is another tool. Maybe the protagonist grew up in this town, went to this school, lived in this house—but now something is wrong. The layout has changed. There's a door that shouldn't be there. The wallpaper is peeling to reveal something underneath.

You don't even need to spell it out—just suggest that the place is shifting, warping, hiding something.

Finally, let the protagonist's **state of mind** infect the setting. If they're paranoid, everything should feel wrong. If they're grieving, the house should feel heavy with loss. If they're unraveling, let the world unravel with them. Readers will pick up on the tension without you ever having to explain it.

The goal is to make the reader look up from your story and glance around their own room, wondering if they missed something in the shadows.

Writing a Great Horror Opening Scene

If you want your horror story to grip readers by the throat from the very first page, you've got to nail the opening scene. In horror, the opening isn't just an introduction—it's the baited hook. It's the cold whisper in the dark that makes the reader lean forward, turn the page, and brace themselves for what's coming.

A great horror opening does three things: it sets the tone, hints at the horror to come, and gives the reader just enough to keep them guessing. It's not about jump scares or cheap thrills. It's about planting a seed of dread that grows with every paragraph.

So let's break down how to craft an opening scene that drags your reader into the nightmare and doesn't let them go.

First, think about **where you want to start.** A common mistake beginner horror writers make is starting too late or too early. You don't need to begin with your protagonist fighting the monster—that's the climax, not the start. But you also don't want to spend three pages describing a sunny day and how normal everything is.

The sweet spot is somewhere in between. Start with a moment that feels normal but unsettling. The reader should sense something's off, even if they can't put their finger on it yet.

For example, maybe your story starts with a couple moving into a new house—but the moving boxes are already unpacked when they arrive. Maybe it starts with a teenager waking up to find muddy footprints in their bedroom. Maybe it starts with an old man in a diner whispering something no one else hears.

You can use ChatGPT to brainstorm these moments fast. Try:

"Give me five unsettling opening scene ideas for a horror story."

Once you have your opening situation, focus on **atmosphere.** You want your first paragraph to ooze tension. Use sensory details—sight, sound, smell, touch. Describe the creak of the floorboards, the cold air on the back of the protagonist's neck, the faint smell of something rotting just out of sight.

You don't need to overdo it. One or two carefully chosen details will do more than a paragraph of purple prose.

A great technique is to open with something **ordinary that feels wrong.** Readers know what a quiet street or an empty room looks like. Show them that—but make it unsettling. Describe how the shadows stretch too far. How the silence presses on the protagonist's ears. How the friendly neighbor won't stop staring.

Another effective trick is to start **in the middle of something.** Drop the reader straight into a conversation, an argument, a small mystery. For example:

"I told you not to go into the basement," she whispered, staring at the dirt on his shoes.

Right away, the reader wants to know: What's in the basement? Why does she look scared?

You can even start with something mundane but ominous. A letter arriving in the mail with no return address. A child's drawing of something horrible. A phone ringing in the middle of the night.

One of the most effective ways to hook your reader is to open with a **question or mystery.** Something the protagonist—or the reader—doesn't understand yet. You're not giving them the monster on page one. You're giving them the sense that the monster is watching, waiting, coming.

You can use ChatGPT to help generate these hooks. Try:

"Write five creepy opening lines for a horror story that create mystery."

Also, don't forget your protagonist. Even if you're starting with a spooky atmosphere or an ominous event, give the reader a reason to care about who's experiencing it. Show a hint of their personality, their flaw, their fear. Readers need to connect with someone to care about what's happening.

Your opening scene should also hint at the **theme** of your story. If your horror story is about isolation, make the protagonist feel alone in the first scene. If it's about guilt, plant a hint of something they regret. If it's about losing control, show them in a situation where things are starting to slip.

And most importantly—don't answer the mystery too soon. Your opening scene should raise questions, not solve them. If you tell the reader exactly what's happening in the first chapter, there's no reason to keep reading.

Think of your opening like the first creak of a door slowly swinging open. You're not showing them what's inside yet—you're letting them feel the cold air leaking out.

Another thing to keep in mind is **pacing.** Your opening scene doesn't need to be action-packed, but it shouldn't drag. Keep the sentences tight. Keep the tension rising. End the scene with a cliffhanger, a question, a moment of dread that forces the reader to turn the page.

You can even use ChatGPT to help structure the scene. Ask:

"Outline a creepy opening scene for a horror story that hints at a supernatural threat."

You'll get a basic structure you can flesh out and personalize.

Lastly, remember that the opening scene is a **promise.** You're telling the reader: "This story will scare you. It will unsettle you. It will crawl under your skin." So make sure you deliver.

Crafting a Nail-Biting Middle Act

If the opening scene of your horror story is the hook, and the ending is the punch in the gut, then the middle act is where you drag your reader kicking and screaming through the darkness. It's the part where everything starts to unravel, where the tension tightens, and where the real terror crawls out from under the bed. The middle act is the heart of your horror story—and if you don't get it right, all the scary stuff at the end won't matter.

So how do you craft a middle act that keeps readers flipping pages, chewing their nails, and wondering if they'll sleep tonight?

Let's break it down.

The middle is where the horror gets personal.

In the first act, your protagonist is introduced, the world feels stable, and the first signs of something wrong creep in. But in the middle, the protagonist realizes this isn't some spooky prank or misunderstanding—this is real, and it's coming for them.

The tension in the middle act comes from **escalation.** Each scene should make things worse. The scares get closer. The body count rises. The protagonist's world starts to crumble. You want the reader to feel like the floor is falling out beneath the characters, piece by piece.

A great tool here is to structure your middle act around **rising stakes.** Start with small, creepy incidents—a door left open, a missing pet, strange noises at night. Then escalate. Someone disappears. The protagonist starts to unravel. The antagonist's presence becomes undeniable.

You can use ChatGPT to help brainstorm this progression. Try:

"Outline five escalating horror scenes for the middle act of a story about a haunted hotel."

You'll get a sequence you can easily adapt.

Character dynamics also drive the middle act. This is where relationships fray. Maybe the protagonist's friends stop believing them. Maybe they argue, turn on each other, or get picked off one by one. The middle act is where alliances break and betrayals sting.

You can make this even more effective by weaving in your characters' **personal fears and flaws.** If your protagonist is terrified of being alone, this is where they get abandoned. If they're running from guilt, this is where the past catches up.

The middle act is also where you reveal pieces of the **backstory and rules** of your horror world—but slowly. You don't want to dump all the information in one scene. Instead, let the protagonist and the reader uncover it bit by bit. A dusty journal, a cryptic warning, a newspaper clipping that hints at something worse.

You can ask ChatGPT to help structure these reveals. Try:

"List five clues the protagonist can find in the middle of a horror story that reveal the monster's backstory."

Another key to a nail-biting middle is the use of **set pieces.** These are your big, terrifying sequences—the scenes readers will remember. A chase through the woods. A séance gone wrong. A friend's horrifying death. You want one or two of these in the middle act to shake up the tension and give the reader something to fear.

Pacing is everything here. You want to keep the tension rising without exhausting the reader. That means balancing quiet, creepy scenes with big, scary moments. Give the reader moments to breathe—but make sure those moments feel uneasy, like the calm before the storm.

One of the best ways to keep the middle act gripping is to raise **questions.** Keep the reader wondering:

- What is really happening?
- Who can be trusted?
- How far will the protagonist go to survive?

And when you answer one question, make sure it raises two more. Every answer should make things worse, not better.

You can use ChatGPT to help generate these mysteries. Try:

"Write five unsettling questions that can be raised in the middle of a horror story."

Also, don't forget to include **foreshadowing** in your middle act. Hint at what's coming without revealing everything. The middle act is where you start setting up your climax. Let the reader feel the noose tightening, but don't let them see how it will snap shut.

Finally, your middle act should end with a **low point.** This is where everything falls apart. The protagonist is broken, hopeless, maybe even defeated. It's the moment that makes the reader think: there's no way out of this.

That's what will make your climax so satisfying—when the protagonist claws their way back from the brink.

Here's a simple formula you can use when pacing your middle act:

Tension → Revelation → Terror → Calm → Bigger Tension → Twist → Hopelessness.

You can use ChatGPT to quickly sketch out this sequence for your specific story.

The middle act is where you show your readers there's no turning back. It's where you make them afraid to turn the page—but unable to stop themselves.

The Climax: How to Write the Big Scare

If the middle act of your horror story is all about tightening the noose, the climax is when you finally pull it tight. This is where everything you've been building toward explodes. It's the big scare, the confrontation, the moment the reader's heart is pounding so hard they can barely keep reading. Your climax is what the entire story has been leading to—and if you get it right, it's the scene your readers will remember long after they close the book.

So how do you write a climax that lands like a punch to the gut?

First, let's be clear about what the climax is. It's not just the scariest scene—it's the **turning point.** The moment when the protagonist faces the monster, the villain, the truth, or their own worst fear. Everything that came before was leading here, and everything after will be shaped by what happens in this moment.

In horror, the climax usually has three key ingredients: **confrontation, escalation, and consequence.**

Confrontation means the protagonist finally comes face to face with the source of the horror. No more running, no more hiding, no more denial. Whether it's a masked killer, a demon, a ghost, or something inside themselves, this is the showdown.

Escalation means the stakes are at their absolute highest. The protagonist is out of options. Their friends are dead, the escape route is blocked, the clock is ticking. The danger is immediate and inescapable.

Consequence means the climax changes everything. Someone dies. The monster is destroyed—or unleashed. The protagonist survives—but not unscathed.

So how do you build this scene?

Start by thinking about your **setting.** A great horror climax uses the setting to its advantage. Maybe it's a burning house, a collapsing tunnel, an empty hospital at night. The place should feel claustrophobic, dangerous, and charged with tension.

You can use ChatGPT to help you flesh this out. Try:

"Describe a terrifying setting for the climax of a horror story about a haunted forest."

Next, think about the **emotional state of your protagonist.** By the time they reach the climax, they should be pushed to their limit. Terrified. Desperate. Broken. Or, maybe they're angry. Determined. Ready to fight.

The climax isn't just about physical survival—it's about what's happening inside the protagonist. Are they facing their greatest fear? Sacrificing something? Confronting a horrible truth?

One of the most powerful tools you can use in the climax is **pacing.** The scene should move fast. Short sentences. Snappy dialogue. No long descriptions. You want the reader to feel breathless, like they're running alongside the protagonist.

You can even structure the climax around a **three-beat sequence**:

1. **Setback:** The protagonist tries something and fails.
2. **Desperation:** They try again, with higher stakes.
3. **Resolution:** They finally succeed—or fail catastrophically.

For example:

- The protagonist tries to shoot the monster—but the gun jams.
- They run, find a hiding spot—but the monster is already there.
- They face it head-on, using the one thing they've been too afraid to use—and win (or lose).

You can ask ChatGPT to help you map this out:

"Outline a three-beat climax sequence for a horror story about a haunted asylum."

Another thing to think about is **surprise.** Your climax should include at least one twist. Maybe the protagonist's friend betrays them. Maybe the monster isn't what it seemed. Maybe the protagonist realizes they've been the villain all along.

But be careful—don't throw in a twist just to shock. It should grow naturally out of the story and tie back to the themes you've been building.

One of the most effective ways to make the climax hit hard is to force the protagonist to make a **terrible choice.** Save themselves or someone else. Kill the monster or become it. Face the truth or live in denial.

You can use ChatGPT to help brainstorm these moments. Try:

"List five difficult choices a horror protagonist could face in the climax."

Finally, when writing the big scare itself—the actual confrontation—lean hard into **sensory detail.** Let the reader hear the scraping of claws on tile, smell the rot in the air, feel the protagonist's racing heartbeat. Keep the prose sharp and immediate. Every line should crackle with tension.

But don't drag it out. A climax that goes on too long loses its power. Once the confrontation starts, move quickly toward the resolution.

And then—end it.

Whether your protagonist survives, escapes, dies, or fails, the climax should leave a mark. The reader should close the book feeling like they've just survived something themselves.

You can even use ChatGPT to help you fine-tune the ending. Try:

"Write a terrifying climax scene for a horror story where the protagonist faces their worst fear."

Then adjust it to fit your characters, setting, and theme.

How to Make the Ending of Your Horror Story Hit Hard

If you've done everything right so far—the creeping dread, the escalating tension, the nail-biting middle, and the terrifying climax—then you're almost there. But the difference between a good horror story and a great one, the one that keeps readers awake at night long after they've finished reading, is the **ending.** The last few lines, the final scene, the lingering question or reveal—that's what stays in the reader's head like a nightmare that won't fade. A horror story's ending should hit hard. It should either give the reader relief, devastation, or a sick twist that leaves them chilled. So let's talk about how to do that.

First, understand the **purpose of a horror ending.**

You're not wrapping things up in a nice little bow. Horror is about discomfort, fear, uncertainty. A good horror ending leaves a scar. Whether your protagonist survives, dies, or something worse, the reader should feel something—shock, dread, heartbreak, or that lingering sense that the horror isn't over.

There are a few ways to structure a horror ending, and you can absolutely use ChatGPT to help you design these quickly when you're writing your story in a day.

1. The "Survivor" Ending

This is one of the most common endings in horror. The protagonist survives the nightmare—but at what cost? They're broken, traumatized, changed forever. Maybe they lost everyone they cared about. Maybe they had to do something terrible to make it out alive.

The key here is not to make survival feel like a victory. Survival in horror should feel heavy.

You can use ChatGPT to help brainstorm:

"Write a bleak but satisfying survivor ending for a horror story."

2. The "No One Gets Out" Ending

The nihilistic horror ending. Everyone dies. Evil wins. The curse continues. This is hard to pull off without leaving the reader feeling hopeless, but when done well, it's devastating and unforgettable.

Think *The Mist* or *Hereditary*. The horror isn't just what happened—it's that it couldn't be stopped.

If you want this kind of ending, make sure it feels **earned.** Don't kill everyone off just to shock the reader. Make it clear, throughout the story, that the odds were stacked against the characters from the start.

3. The "Twist" Ending

Horror loves a last-minute twist. The protagonist thinks they've won—but the monster isn't dead. The curse is still active. The person they saved isn't really who they thought. The danger isn't over.

You can use ChatGPT to help brainstorm these twists fast. Try:

"Give me five shocking twist endings for a horror story."

Just be careful—don't twist for the sake of twisting. Make sure the seeds of the twist are planted earlier in the story, so it feels surprising but inevitable.

4. The "Open-Ended" Ending

Leave the reader with a question. Don't explain everything. Let the horror linger in ambiguity. Did the protagonist survive? Was it all in their head? Is the horror still out there? This kind of ending works well if your story has been playing with perception, unreliable narration, or psychological horror.

5. The "Resolution with a Sting" Ending

This is the classic "the nightmare is over... or is it?" ending. The protagonist escapes. The villain is dead. The curse is lifted. And then, in the last line or scene, you reveal that something is still wrong. Maybe the protagonist hears a familiar whisper. Maybe there's a reflection in the mirror that shouldn't be there. Maybe a new character unknowingly picks up the cursed object. That final sting sends the reader off with a shiver.

How to Make It Hit Hard

No matter what ending you choose, there are a few things you can do to make it land:

Make It Personal

The ending should tie back to your protagonist's journey. If the story was about their fear of being alone, the ending should leave them isolated—or finally surrounded by people, but unable to connect. If the story was about guilt, the ending should force them to live with what they've done.

Pay Off Your Themes

Whatever themes you've been weaving through your story—loss, isolation, survival, the darkness within—your ending should drive them home. Let the horror resonate on a deeper level than just scares.

End on a Strong Image or Line

The last sentence of your horror story is your last chance to leave an impression. Make it sharp, chilling, or thought-provoking. Leave the reader staring at the page.

You can ask ChatGPT to help you write this:

"Write five final lines for a horror story that leave the reader unsettled."

Don't Explain Too Much

The scariest horror endings leave questions. Don't explain every detail. Let the reader wonder what happened after the final scene. Let them fill in the blanks with their own worst fears.

Let It Linger

The best horror endings don't close the door—they leave it ajar. They make the reader check the shadows. They make them wonder what's lurking in the dark corners of the story—and maybe in their own home.

Using ChatGPT to Write Killer Descriptions

One of the things that makes horror so powerful is how it makes you **feel** things. You don't just read a horror story—you experience it. You feel the chill crawling up your spine, the dread pooling in your stomach, the panic when the lights go out. And a huge part of that comes down to **description.** The words you choose to paint the scene, describe the horror, and drag the reader into the nightmare.

But writing killer descriptions isn't always easy—especially when you're trying to write an entire horror story in a day. That's where ChatGPT becomes your best friend.

In this chapter, we're going to talk about how to use ChatGPT to generate vivid, terrifying, sensory-rich descriptions that will make your story jump off the page and claw its way into the reader's imagination.

First, let's talk about what makes a great horror description.

1. Sensory Detail

Horror is a physical experience. You want your reader to hear the creak of the floorboards, smell the mildew in the air, feel the cold breath on their neck. The more senses you can engage, the more real the horror feels.

When you're writing fast, you don't always have time to think of the perfect smell, sound, or texture. That's where ChatGPT comes in handy. You can type something like:

"Describe a haunted basement using sensory details."

You'll get back a paragraph like:

The basement smelled of damp earth and rusted metal. The air was thick, heavy, and cold against her skin. Every footstep echoed too loud, and something dripped steadily in the darkness, though she couldn't see what.

That's a ready-to-go description you can drop straight into your story—or tweak to match your style.

2. Atmosphere Over Information

One mistake a lot of horror writers make is describing everything. You don't need to list every crack in the wall or every piece of furniture. You want to describe just enough to make the reader feel the mood.

Horror descriptions should lean into atmosphere. Is the scene oppressive? Cold? Claustrophobic? Dangerous? ChatGPT can help you quickly generate these atmospheric touches. Try:

"Write a description of an abandoned hospital that feels oppressive and threatening."

You'll get something like:

The hospital's hallways stretched endlessly, lined with flickering lights and peeling paint. Every door hung ajar, like mouths frozen mid-scream. The air smelled faintly of bleach and something rotten.

Quick, effective, and drenched in mood.

3. Suggestion Over Explanation

Horror lives in what you don't show. When you describe something horrifying, the best strategy is to give enough detail to let the reader's imagination do the rest.

Instead of writing:

"The monster had yellow eyes, sharp teeth, long claws, and a hunched back."

Try something more suggestive:

"It crouched in the shadows, its yellow eyes catching the light like coins at the bottom of a dark well. Something sharp flashed when it smiled."

You can use ChatGPT to help rephrase descriptions to make them more suggestive and unsettling. Try:

"Rewrite this monster description to be more mysterious and creepy."

4. Dynamic Descriptions

Your descriptions shouldn't stop the action—they should be part of it. In horror, pacing is everything. So make your descriptions work double-duty by keeping them short, sharp, and tense.

For example:

The door groaned open, spilling cold air into the room like a warning.

Her fingers brushed against something wet and warm in the dark—something that twitched when she touched it.

You can ask ChatGPT:

"Write short, dynamic descriptions for a tense horror scene."

This will give you quick snippets you can sprinkle throughout your story without slowing things down.

5. Character-Centric Description

Make sure your descriptions reflect how your protagonist experiences the scene. If they're panicking, your descriptions should feel chaotic. If they're trying to stay calm, the descriptions might focus on small, distracting details.

For example:

The clock on the wall ticked too loud, like a heartbeat counting down to something terrible.

You can ask ChatGPT:

"Describe a haunted house through the eyes of a terrified protagonist."

This gives you not just a visual, but an emotional lens.

How to Use ChatGPT Effectively

Here's how you can use ChatGPT in real-time as you're writing your horror story in one day:

- When you hit a scene and need a creepy setting, type:
  "Describe an eerie abandoned motel."
- When you need sensory detail:
  "List five creepy sounds that could be heard in a haunted forest."
- When you want a sharp line to end a scene:
  "Write a chilling final sentence for a horror scene."
- When you want to describe a monster without overexplaining:
  "Describe a monster in vague, terrifying terms without showing too much."

You can even get ChatGPT to help you rewrite your own descriptions to make them scarier, faster, or more atmospheric.

Why This Works

The beauty of using ChatGPT for descriptions is that it saves you time and creative energy. Instead of getting stuck trying to find the perfect adjective, you can generate a dozen options in seconds and pick the one that fits your tone.

And because you're writing your horror story in one day, speed matters. ChatGPT lets you move fast without sacrificing atmosphere, mood, or detail.

Weaving in Symbolism and Subtext in Horror

One of the reasons the best horror stories stay with people long after the last page isn't just because of the scares—it's because there's **something underneath.** The monsters mean something. The darkness isn't just darkness. The characters' struggles echo bigger, more universal fears. That's where **symbolism** and **subtext** come in.

You don't need to beat your readers over the head with "deep meaning" in a horror story. In fact, the best horror symbolism is subtle. It works under the surface, creeping into the reader's mind without them even realizing it.

So let's talk about how you can weave symbolism and subtext into your horror story—even when you're writing it in one day, with the help of ChatGPT.

First, understand the difference. **Symbolism** is when an object, person, or event stands for something bigger. A rotting house might symbolize a crumbling family. A creeping fog might represent depression. A monster might stand in for guilt, grief, or trauma.

Subtext is the meaning that isn't spoken outright. It's the tension in a conversation, the thing the character won't say, the fear beneath the surface.

Both of these make your horror story richer, deeper, and more memorable.

Why Use Symbolism in Horror?

Because horror is about fear—and the scariest fears aren't about ghosts or monsters. They're about losing control. About death. About grief, shame, trauma, guilt, loneliness. When you give your horror story a layer of symbolism, you tap into those deeper fears.

Think about movies like *The Babadook*—where the monster is clearly a metaphor for grief and depression. Or *Get Out*—where the horror is a reflection of racism and exploitation. Or *The Shining*—which is as much about isolation and addiction as it is about ghosts.

The monster matters. But what it **means** is what makes the story linger.

How to Add Symbolism without Slowing Down

You're writing this story in one day, so you don't have time to craft a literary masterpiece. But you can still sprinkle in symbolism as you go.

One easy way is to pick an object, place, or image and give it extra weight. Maybe your protagonist keeps seeing dead birds, symbolizing death and decay. Maybe the setting itself—a decaying town, an empty hospital—mirrors the protagonist's emotional state.

You can even use ChatGPT to help brainstorm this fast. Try:

"List ten symbolic objects or images that could be used in a horror story about guilt."

You'll get ideas like broken mirrors, bloodstains that won't wash away, recurring dreams of falling.

Using Subtext in Dialogue and Scenes

Subtext is all about what's **not** being said. In horror, this is gold. Your characters are scared, but they won't always admit it. They're hiding things, denying things, lying to themselves.

For example, instead of writing:

"I'm terrified," she said.

Use subtext:

"She laughed too loud, fingers twitching as she locked the door behind her."

The reader knows she's scared without being told.

You can ask ChatGPT to help you sharpen your dialogue. Try:

"Rewrite this conversation to include more tension and subtext in a horror story."

Themes and Symbolism Go Hand-in-Hand

When you're writing your horror story, you should already have a theme in mind. Maybe it's about grief, isolation, guilt, or the darkness within. Whatever it is, you can use symbolism to reinforce that theme without spelling it out.

If your theme is about isolation, let the world around the protagonist reflect that. Empty streets. Silent rooms. Characters who won't answer their phone calls.

If it's about guilt, make the horror **personal.** The monster knows the protagonist's secret. The setting reminds them of something they've done.

You can ask ChatGPT to help you brainstorm:

"List five ways to use setting and symbolism to reinforce the theme of guilt in a horror story."

Don't Overdo It

Symbolism works best when it's subtle. Readers don't want to feel like they're reading a lecture on grief, trauma, or loneliness—they want to feel scared. Your job is to make them uncomfortable **and** make them think.

The best horror stories make readers feel something bigger without being obvious. They leave the reader wondering, hours later, "Was that monster really about something more?"

Practical Ways to Add Symbolism Quickly

Since you're writing this in a single day, here's a shortcut:

Once you've outlined your story (which we'll cover more in upcoming chapters), go back and look at your characters, setting, and antagonist. Pick one or two things you can layer in symbolically. A recurring image. A line of dialogue. A character's habit.

You don't need to rewrite your whole story. You just need to sprinkle in enough to give the reader something to chew on.

And when you get stuck, use ChatGPT. Ask for symbolism ideas based on your story's theme. Ask for subtext-rich dialogue. Ask for imagery that reflects the protagonist's fears.

The more layers you can add, the more your horror story will stick in the reader's mind—not just because it scared them, but because it said something about fear itself.

Writing Gore without Going Overboard

Let's talk about gore. Blood, guts, broken bones, rotting flesh—all the squishy, nasty details that make readers cringe, squirm, or even close the book for a moment because it's just too much. Gore is part of the horror tradition, no doubt about it. Some readers expect it. Some writers love it. But if you're not careful, too much gore can ruin your story.

Gore in horror is like seasoning. A little goes a long way. Pour too much in, and you're not scaring your reader—you're grossing them out, or worse, boring them. So in this chapter, we're going to break down how to use gore effectively, how to know when enough is enough, and how to write bloody, brutal scenes without losing your readers.

First, let's get something clear—**gore is not horror.** Horror is about fear, tension, dread, and the unknown. Gore is just one tool you can use to make things feel visceral and real. It can be shocking. It can be disturbing. But it's never enough to carry a story by itself.

If you rely too heavily on gore without building atmosphere, character, and tension, readers will tune out. They'll either get numb to the violence, or they'll feel like you're trying too hard to shock them without giving them anything to care about.

So how do you use gore the right way?

1. Make It Serve the Story

The most important rule is: **Gore should mean something.** Don't throw in a bloody scene just to gross people out. The violence should either move the plot forward, reveal something about the characters, or hit the reader emotionally.

For example, a character's death scene is way more powerful if the protagonist is helpless to stop it—or worse, responsible for it. A graphic injury is more horrifying if it forces the character to keep going despite the pain.

You can use ChatGPT to help structure these moments. Try:

"Outline a gory horror scene where the violence reveals something about the protagonist."

2. Less Is More

Sometimes, what you **don't** show is scarier. You can describe the aftermath instead of the act itself—the blood trail, the broken body, the protagonist's reaction. Readers' imaginations will fill in the blanks, often making it worse than anything you could write.

A classic example: In *Psycho*, you never actually see the knife stabbing flesh in the shower scene. But it's one of the most famous, terrifying scenes in film history because of how it's shot, edited, and implied.

3. Focus on the Senses

If you're going to describe gore, make it visceral. Don't just say, "Blood was everywhere." Make the reader feel it. The slick warmth on the protagonist's hands. The metallic taste in their mouth. The smell of copper and rot.

You can use ChatGPT to help you sharpen these descriptions fast. Try:

"Describe a gory horror scene using all five senses."

But again—don't go overboard. A paragraph of blood and guts is effective. Three pages of it is exhausting.

4. Know Your Audience and Subgenre

Some horror readers love splatterpunk—stories where the gore is the point. Others prefer psychological horror with barely any violence. If you're writing a slasher story, you can get away with more gore than if you're writing a haunted house story. Think about what kind of horror you're writing, and how much gore your readers expect. If you're writing a fast, brutal survival story, you can lean in. If you're writing slow-burn atmospheric horror, too much blood might kill the mood.

5. Use Gore to Escalate Tension

One of the best ways to use gore is to show how bad things are getting. The first death might be subtle. The second, brutal. By the time you hit the climax, you can let things get messy—but by then, the reader is already invested.

You can ask ChatGPT to help you structure this escalation:

"Outline three gory scenes in a horror story, each one more intense than the last."

6. Keep the Reader's Focus on the Characters

The difference between good gore and bad gore is emotional impact. Readers won't care about a random stranger getting disembowelled. But if it's a character they know, love, or hate, the violence hits harder. When you're writing a gory scene, make sure the reader is in the protagonist's head. Show how they feel, how they react. Make the violence personal.

7. Don't Let Gore Distract from the Fear

Remember, fear is what makes horror work—not blood. If your story is just a parade of gruesome scenes with no tension, no atmosphere, and no emotional weight, the reader will get bored.

Use gore like a jump scare. It should be shocking, but it should also mean something and fit within a larger story that's built on dread, suspense, and fear.

Quick ChatGPT Trick

If you want to write a gory scene but aren't sure how far to go, you can ask ChatGPT:

"Write three versions of a gory horror scene—one subtle, one intense, one extreme."

Then you can choose the level that fits your story and audience.

Final Tip

When you're editing your story after that one-day writing blitz, pay attention to the gore. Ask yourself:

- Does this scene need to be this graphic?
- Is the violence serving the story, or is it just shock value?
- Will this scene land harder if I imply more and show less?

Sometimes, trimming a sentence or cutting a graphic detail will make the scene more powerful.

Creating Realistic Reactions to Horror Events

One of the quickest ways to ruin a great horror story is to fill it with characters who react unrealistically. You've seen it in bad horror movies—the guy who runs toward the sound in the basement, the friend who laughs off obvious danger, the protagonist who shows no emotion after watching someone die horribly. It kills the tension and breaks the reader's immersion.

If you want your horror story to really hit, your characters' reactions need to feel real. Readers need to believe that if **they** were in that situation, they'd feel the same panic, confusion, shock, or even numbness.

In this chapter, we'll talk about how to craft authentic, believable reactions to terrifying events—and how to use ChatGPT to help you pull it off fast.

Why Realistic Reactions Matter

Horror is emotional. If your characters don't react to the horror around them, the reader won't either. It doesn't matter how scary the monster is, how bloody the murder scene, or how terrifying the atmosphere—if your characters shrug it off or act like robots, the tension disappears.

Realistic reactions make the horror personal. They pull the reader deeper into the story because they can relate to the fear, panic, or shock.

Common Emotional Responses in Horror

When something terrifying happens, characters don't just scream and run. People react to fear in all kinds of ways—some obvious, some surprising. Here are a few common reactions you can use:

- **Panic:** Fast breathing, racing heart, irrational decisions.
- **Shock:** Numbness, inability to speak, going still.
- **Denial:** Laughing, brushing it off, pretending nothing's wrong.
- **Freeze Response:** Some people literally freeze when scared.
- **Anger:** Lashing out, yelling, blaming others.
- **Tears:** Crying isn't weak—it's a real, human response to terror.
- **Fight Response:** Going on the attack, even recklessly.
- **Flight Response:** Running away without a plan.
- **Hyper-awareness:** Hearing every sound, noticing tiny details.

You can use ChatGPT to help you quickly write these reactions. Try:

"Describe a realistic fear response when a character sees a ghost."

Physical Reactions

Your characters' bodies should react too. Don't just tell the reader they're scared—show it through body language and sensory detail:

- Cold sweat
- Shaking hands
- Short, shallow breathing
- Dry mouth
- Tightening stomach
- Racing heartbeat
- Goosebumps
- Stumbling or clumsiness

For example:

"Her hands trembled as she fumbled with the lock, breath coming in sharp, shallow bursts. Her heartbeat thundered in her ears, drowning out the scratching sound on the other side of the door."

Emotional Layers

Real fear isn't just about the moment—it's about what's underneath. A character might react differently to horror if they're already grieving, angry, guilty, or traumatized. Think about what's going on inside your protagonist's head and let that shape their reactions.

If your protagonist is terrified of being alone, seeing their friend murdered might trigger panic, but also a crushing sense of abandonment. If they've been denying the danger up until now, the moment they finally realize it's real might hit like a ton of bricks.

You can ask ChatGPT to help layer these emotions:

"Write a scene where a horror protagonist reacts to seeing their best friend killed, showing shock, grief, and fear."

Coping Mechanisms

Not all reactions to horror are immediate. Some characters will break down hours or days later. Some will joke, deny, or try to take control. Others will spiral into paranoia or recklessness.

Think about how your characters **cope** with the horror. Do they bottle it up? Snap at others? Become hyper-vigilant? Your story will feel richer and more realistic if their emotional responses continue after the scary scene is over.

Group Dynamics

If your horror story has a group of characters, show how their reactions bounce off each other. Fear isn't experienced in a vacuum. One character might panic while another tries to take charge. Someone might get angry, someone might shut down.

Tension between characters adds an extra layer of horror. Readers aren't just afraid of the monster—they're afraid of what the characters will do when pushed to the edge.

The "Wrong" Reaction Can Be Terrifying

Sometimes, the scariest reaction is no reaction at all. A character who doesn't flinch when something horrifying happens—a kid who keeps drawing creepy pictures after witnessing a murder, a protagonist who stops caring whether they live or die—can be unsettling.

If you want to play with this, make sure it's intentional and tied to the story. Readers should wonder why the character is numb or detached—and fear what it means.

Quick Reaction Templates with ChatGPT

When you're writing your horror story in one day, you don't have time to agonize over every reaction scene. So use ChatGPT to speed things up. Try prompts like:

- **"Write three different character reactions to finding a dead body."**
- **"Describe how a character might react physically and emotionally after surviving an attack."**
- **"Give five ways a horror protagonist could react to being hunted by a monster."**

You can copy, paste, tweak, and personalize these responses as you go.

Don't Forget the Aftermath

The best horror stories don't stop at the scare. Show how the event lingers. Let the character flinch at shadows, lose sleep, lash out at friends, question their sanity. Realistic horror reactions don't end when the danger passes—they haunt the character long after.

The Power of Isolation and Helplessness

If there's one thing that will supercharge the terror in your horror story, it's the feeling of being completely, utterly **alone**. Not just physically, but mentally, emotionally, and psychologically cut off from any help, hope, or safety. Isolation and helplessness are two of the sharpest knives in your horror toolbox, and when you use them right, you don't even need a monster to make your readers squirm.

Why? Because human beings are wired to fear abandonment, vulnerability, and being trapped. Horror stories that lean into these feelings work not just because something scary is happening—but because the protagonist has **no one and nowhere to turn.**

In this chapter, we're going to talk about how to use isolation and helplessness to make your horror story hit harder—and how to use ChatGPT to brainstorm the most chilling ways to trap your characters.

Physical Isolation

The most obvious kind of isolation is physical. Your protagonist is literally cut off from the world. No phone signal. No car. No help coming. This is why so many horror stories are set in remote cabins, creepy forests, abandoned hospitals, or small towns where no one's left.

You can make this isolation worse by taking away the protagonist's control. Maybe their car breaks down. Maybe a snowstorm hits. Maybe the roads are blocked. Whatever you choose, make sure the reader knows: **no one is coming to help.**

You can ask ChatGPT to help brainstorm these scenarios fast. Try:

"List five ways to physically isolate a protagonist in a horror story."

You'll get ideas like:

- A snowstorm cuts off all roads and communication.
- The protagonist wakes up in an underground bunker with no way out.
- An island getaway turns into a nightmare when the boat disappears.
- A small town shuts its gates and won't let anyone leave.
- A power outage traps the protagonist in an abandoned asylum.

Emotional Isolation

Physical isolation is scary—but emotional isolation cuts deeper. Even if the protagonist is surrounded by people, they can feel utterly alone. Maybe no one believes them. Maybe their friends turn on them. Maybe they've lost everyone they love, and now they're facing the horror alone.

You can layer this into your story by making sure the protagonist has no support system. When they tell someone about the ghost, the demon, or the monster, no one listens. When they reach out for help, no one answers. That creeping sense of being **unseen, unheard, and abandoned** can be more terrifying than any physical threat.

You can ask ChatGPT:

"List five ways to emotionally isolate a protagonist in a horror story."

Psychological Isolation

This is the kind of isolation that really messes with the reader's head. It's when the protagonist starts to doubt their own sanity. Maybe the horror only appears to them. Maybe they can't tell what's real and what's a nightmare. Maybe the thing they're fighting is inside their own mind.

Psychological isolation makes the protagonist—and the reader—feel helpless because there's no one to trust, not even themselves.

If you want to use this, ask ChatGPT:

"List five ways to make a horror protagonist question their sanity."

Helplessness: Turning the Screws

Isolation sets the stage—but helplessness is what turns up the pressure. Your protagonist doesn't just feel alone—they feel **powerless.** The horror is bigger than them. They can't fight it. They can't escape. They can't even understand it.

You can create helplessness by:

- Making the antagonist stronger, smarter, or faster.
- Taking away the protagonist's resources (no weapons, no allies, no way out).
- Giving the protagonist a weakness—an injury, a phobia, a secret—that the horror exploits.
- Trapping them in an impossible situation (protect a loved one or save themselves, fight or run, believe what they see or go mad).

The more powerless the protagonist feels, the scarier the story becomes.

You can use ChatGPT to help create these scenarios quickly:

"Describe three situations in a horror story where the protagonist feels completely helpless."

Pacing Isolation and Helplessness

One important thing to remember: you want to **build** isolation and helplessness over time. Don't start your story with the protagonist totally alone and powerless—that gives you nowhere to go. Instead, start with small cracks. A phone call that doesn't go through. A friend who stops answering. A door that locks behind them.

Scene by scene, make things worse. Every time the protagonist tries to fix things, they fail. Every time they reach out, the door slams shut. By the time you hit the climax, the reader should feel like the protagonist has no hope left.

The Psychological Payoff

Isolation and helplessness aren't just plot devices—they're emotional gut punches. When the protagonist finally fights back—or doesn't—the payoff will be bigger because the reader felt every step of their descent into terror.

If your protagonist survives, it's because they found strength when they had nothing left. If they die, the reader will feel the weight of that helplessness. Either way, the ending will hit harder.

Quick ChatGPT Trick

If you want to build isolation and helplessness into your outline fast, ask:

"Outline five key moments in a horror story where the protagonist becomes increasingly isolated and helpless."

You'll get a ready-made sequence you can plug straight into your story.

How to Keep the Reader Guessing

If there's one thing that separates a **forgettable** horror story from a **great** one, it's this: The reader never knows what's coming next. Horror is built on uncertainty, dread, and the creeping fear that the ground beneath your feet is about to collapse. If your reader can predict every twist, scare, and reveal, they won't feel scared—they'll feel bored.

So how do you keep your reader guessing, especially when you're writing your horror story quickly, in one day, with the help of ChatGPT? It all comes down to how you control **information, pacing, and expectation.**

Let's break it down.

1. Withhold Information (But Give Enough to Keep Them Hooked)

One of the simplest ways to keep your reader guessing is to **not tell them everything.** Horror thrives on mystery. Who is the killer? Why is the house haunted? What's hiding in the basement?

You want your reader to ask questions on every page—but you need to give them just enough clues to keep them hungry for answers.

Think of it like breadcrumbs. Drop enough to lead them deeper into the woods, but never show them the whole picture until it's too late.

You can use ChatGPT to help you structure this:

"Outline a horror story with three major secrets that are revealed gradually."

2. Use Red Herrings

A classic tool in horror (and mystery) is the **red herring**—something that looks important but isn't. Maybe a creepy neighbor who seems suspicious but is actually harmless. Maybe a series of clues that lead the protagonist down the wrong path.

Red herrings keep your reader second-guessing everything. Just make sure you don't overdo it. If every clue is a fake-out, the reader will get frustrated. But one or two well-placed misdirections can add serious tension.

You can ask ChatGPT to help you brainstorm these:

"List five red herring characters or clues for a psychological horror story."

3. Make Your Characters Unreliable

One of the best ways to keep readers guessing is to make them question what's real. An **unreliable narrator**—someone who's lying, hallucinating, or in denial—can turn the entire story upside down.

Maybe your protagonist is losing their mind. Maybe they're hiding something. Maybe their perspective is skewed by grief, guilt, or trauma.

If you want to play with this, you can use ChatGPT to help layer it in:

"Write a scene where a horror protagonist questions if what they're seeing is real."

4. Break the Rules

Readers who love horror stories have seen it all. They know the tropes. So one way to keep them guessing is to **break the rules.**

- Kill off a character they thought was safe.
- Reveal the monster halfway through, not at the end.
- Let the protagonist fail.
- End a chapter on a fake scare—then hit them with the real one.

Every time your reader thinks they know what's happening, flip it.

5. Pacing and Structure

You can also use pacing to keep readers off-balance. Alternate between slow, creeping dread and fast, chaotic terror. Lull the reader into a false sense of security, then pull the rug out from under them.

Try ending chapters with a cliffhanger, a shocking revelation, or a question that forces them to keep reading.

You can use ChatGPT to help with this structure:

"Outline five chapter endings in a horror story that will leave readers wanting to know what happens next."

6. Add Layers of Mystery

A simple scare is fine—but a **mystery** keeps readers guessing. Why is the monster hunting them? Why did the town vanish overnight? Why is the protagonist the only one who can see the ghost?

The more questions your story raises, the more invested your readers will be in finding the answers. Just make sure you actually answer the big ones—nothing kills a horror story faster than leaving too many loose threads.

7. The "Twist You Didn't See Coming"

A well-placed twist can change the entire story. Maybe the protagonist was the villain all along. Maybe the monster doesn't exist—it's all in their head. Maybe the person they trusted is the real threat.

A twist works best when the clues were there all along, but the reader didn't notice them until it's too late.

You can use ChatGPT to help brainstorm:

"List five unexpected twists for a horror story that will shock the reader."

The Key: Balance

It's tempting to throw in twist after twist, but too much unpredictability can make your story feel chaotic or cheap. The trick is to balance mystery with tension. You want the reader to think they know what's happening—until they realize they don't.

A good horror story is like a maze. The reader keeps thinking they're about to find the exit—but every turn leads somewhere darker.

Practical Tip

When you're outlining your horror story (which we'll cover in more detail soon), make a list of what the reader knows at each stage—and what they **don't** know yet. Use that list to control the flow of information. That's how you keep them guessing without confusing them.

Quick ChatGPT Trick

When you're writing and need to throw the reader off balance, type:

"Write a scene where a horror protagonist thinks they're safe—but they're not."

You'll get a ready-made moment of dread you can drop into your story.

Developing Conflict and Tension Scene by Scene

If you want your horror story to grab the reader and never let go, you need one thing running through every page: **conflict and tension.** These two elements are the fuel that keeps the horror fire burning. It's not enough to have one or two scary scenes—you need tension baked into every scene, every conversation, every moment.

And the secret to doing that, especially when you're writing a story in a single day with ChatGPT, is knowing how to develop conflict and tension **scene by scene.** That's what we're going to break down right here.

What's the Difference between Conflict and Tension?

First, let's get clear on what we're talking about.

Conflict is about obstacles. It's what stands in the protagonist's way—whether that's a monster, a person, or their own fears.

Tension is about uncertainty. It's the feeling that something bad is about to happen, that things could explode at any moment.

Your story needs both.

Scene-Level Conflict

Every scene should have conflict. That doesn't mean there has to be a physical fight or a chase scene every five minutes. Conflict can be small and subtle, but it has to be there.

Here's how you can create scene-level conflict quickly and effectively:

1. **Character vs. Character**
   This is the most obvious. Arguments, fights, betrayals. Even something as small as one character lying to another creates conflict.
2. **Character vs. Environment**
   The protagonist is lost in the woods. The storm is closing in. The haunted house is falling apart. The world itself is against them.
3. **Character vs. Self**
   Internal conflict is huge in horror. The protagonist is scared, guilty, traumatized, or doubting themselves. Even when nothing's happening outside, they're at war inside.
4. **Character vs. Supernatural/Unknown**
   The monster, the curse, the thing lurking just out of sight. This is the obvious external conflict—but you can layer it in slowly, scene by scene.

You can use ChatGPT to help you brainstorm scene-level conflicts fast. Try:

"List five small but tense conflicts that could happen between characters in a horror story."

Building Tension Scene by Scene

Tension is all about **anticipation.** What might happen. The key is to never let the reader feel safe. Every scene should leave a little question hanging in the air.

Here's how you can structure tension:

Start Each Scene with a Question

Before you write a scene, ask yourself:

What is the reader wondering right now?

What is the character afraid of in this moment?

Maybe the question is:

- Will they find their missing friend?
- Is the neighbor hiding something?
- What's making that sound upstairs?

You can even use ChatGPT to help you list these questions as you outline. Try:

"List five tension-building questions to use in a horror story."

End Each Scene on a Hook

Don't let scenes fizzle out. End with a cliffhanger, a shock, a new mystery, or a creeping sense of dread. Make the reader want—need—to turn the page.

You can ask ChatGPT:

"Write five horror scene endings that leave readers in suspense."

Escalate Every Scene

Each scene should raise the stakes. The conflict should get bigger. The tension should tighten. The protagonist should lose ground, lose allies, lose hope.

Think of your scenes like a staircase leading down into darkness. Each step takes the reader deeper, until there's no way back.

How to Layer Conflict and Tension Quickly

Since you're writing this story fast, you can use a simple strategy to map your tension and conflict:

1. **Outline your scenes.**
2. For each scene, ask:
    - What's the conflict here?
    - How can I make the protagonist uncomfortable?
    - How can I end the scene on a hook?
3. Use ChatGPT to help fill in gaps. For example:
   "Outline the tension and conflict in a scene where a protagonist is trapped in a haunted hotel room."

Types of Tension You Can Use

If you want variety, here's a quick cheat sheet of different tension types you can build scene by scene:

- **Physical tension:** The protagonist is in immediate danger.
- **Emotional tension:** Relationships are strained, secrets revealed.
- **Psychological tension:** The protagonist doubts their own sanity.
- **Mystery tension:** A new clue or question emerges.
- **Moral tension:** The protagonist faces an impossible choice.

You can weave these together to keep the reader on edge without exhausting them with non-stop action.

Quick ChatGPT Trick

When you're writing and feel like a scene is falling flat, ask:

"How can I add more conflict and tension to this scene?"

You'll get immediate suggestions to spice things up.

The Rule of No Comfort Zones

Here's a simple rule to remember as you build conflict and tension: **Never let your protagonist feel safe.**

Even when things calm down, let the reader feel the dread creeping back in. A character might relax—but something's always lurking in the shadows.

How to Balance Horror and Mystery

One of the secret weapons of a truly great horror story is how well it balances two forces—**horror and mystery.** These two work together like a one-two punch. The horror grabs your reader by the throat, and the mystery keeps them turning the page, desperate to find out what's really going on. When you get that balance right, you don't just scare your readers—you hook them.

But if you lean too much into horror without mystery, you risk writing a shallow gore-fest that shocks but doesn't linger. And if you load up on mystery without delivering the fear, you might write an intriguing thriller—but it won't terrify anyone.

So in this chapter, we're going to break down how to blend both and how to use ChatGPT to make it happen fast, even when you're writing your story in one day.

Understanding the Difference

First, let's quickly define what we're working with:

Horror is about the emotional experience. It's about fear, dread, terror, tension, and sometimes gore. It's what makes the reader feel uncomfortable.

Mystery is about information. It's about questions, secrets, puzzles, and figuring out what's really happening. It's what keeps the reader curious.

The sweet spot in horror writing is when you keep readers emotionally terrified **and** mentally engaged.

How Horror and Mystery Work Together

Think about some of the best horror stories you've seen or read. *The Ring*, *Hereditary*, *The Blair Witch Project*, *The Others*, *The Babadook*—all of these blend horror and mystery masterfully.

You're not just scared of the monster or the ghost—you're dying to know:

- What is it?
- Where did it come from?
- How can it be stopped?
- Why is this happening?

The mystery drives the plot forward. The horror makes every step terrifying.

How to Structure the Balance

A simple way to structure this balance is to layer the mystery **under** the horror.

Start with something terrifying: a death, a haunting, a gruesome discovery. But don't explain it. Drop hints, suggest connections, leave questions unanswered.

Each time the protagonist learns something new, the horror should escalate. As the mystery unravels, the danger increases.

You can use ChatGPT to help structure this easily. Try:

"Outline a horror story where a supernatural mystery is revealed piece by piece."

Start with a Core Question

A great horror mystery starts with a simple, unsettling question.

- Why are people disappearing?
- Why is the protagonist seeing things no one else can?
- Why does the house make people go mad?

That question drives the narrative. The horror makes every step toward the answer terrifying.

You can ask ChatGPT:

"List five creepy mystery questions that could drive a horror story."

Use Clues and Red Herrings

A strong mystery needs clues—and misdirection. Feed your protagonist (and reader) information slowly. Let them piece it together. But also throw in false leads, dead ends, or hints that seem important but aren't.

This keeps your readers guessing and amps up the tension.

You can use ChatGPT to brainstorm these quickly:

"List five red herring clues in a horror story about a cursed town."

Reveal the Mystery at the Right Time

The biggest mistake horror writers make is revealing the mystery too early—or too late.

If you reveal the answers too soon, the tension evaporates. If you hold off too long, the reader gets frustrated.

The ideal structure is to let the reader figure out **pieces** of the mystery as the horror escalates—but hold back the biggest reveal for the climax.

Tie the Horror to the Mystery

The mystery shouldn't feel like a separate subplot. It should be directly connected to the horror.

Maybe the monster is tied to a dark secret. Maybe the protagonist's personal trauma is part of the curse. Maybe the mystery reveals that the protagonist is the real danger.

The more personal and connected the mystery is to the horror, the stronger your story will be.

You can ask ChatGPT to help tie these together:

"Suggest five ways to connect a horror mystery to the protagonist's backstory."

Don't Over-Explain

One of the best things about horror mysteries is the unanswered question. Don't explain everything. Leave some shadows unexplored.

A little ambiguity makes the story linger in the reader's mind.

Think of movies like *The Blair Witch Project* or *It Follows*—you never fully understand the horror, and that makes it scarier.

Quick ChatGPT Trick

When you're writing your horror story, you can use ChatGPT to quickly balance horror and mystery. Try:

"Outline five scenes in a horror story where new information is revealed while the tension escalates."

This will help you structure your story so the mystery unravels and the horror ramps up at the same time.

Final Thought

The perfect horror story isn't just about making readers scream. It's about making them **wonder.** When you keep them guessing **and** terrified, you'll have them flipping pages long after midnight.

The Role of the Supernatural in Your Story

If there's one element that's defined the horror genre for centuries, it's the **supernatural.** Ghosts, demons, curses, monsters from beyond the veil—it's the stuff that fuels nightmares and keeps readers turning the page. But the supernatural in a horror story isn't just about jump scares or flashy effects. It plays a much deeper role. It's there to unsettle, to disrupt, to symbolize, and to confront both the characters and the reader with something that can't be explained away.

In this chapter, we're going to break down how to use the supernatural in your horror story and how you can leverage ChatGPT to help you build terrifying supernatural elements fast, even when you're writing your story in one day.

What Does "Supernatural" Really Mean in Horror?

The supernatural, at its core, is anything **outside the natural order.** Ghosts, demons, vampires, eldritch entities, cursed objects, unexplainable events—anything that breaks the rules of the world as we know it.

But here's the key: the supernatural in horror isn't just for decoration. It's not about the monster. It's about what the monster **represents.** It's about what the unexplainable does to the characters—and how it forces them to confront their deepest fears.

Decide What the Supernatural Means in Your Story

Before you start throwing ghosts and demons around, ask yourself:

What is the supernatural element really about?

Is it about grief, guilt, trauma, fear of death, fear of the unknown, loss of control?

Think about horror classics like *The Babadook* (grief), *The Shining* (isolation and addiction), or *It Follows* (sexual guilt and trauma). The supernatural forces aren't just random—they're tied directly to the protagonist's personal demons.

You can use ChatGPT to brainstorm this connection fast. Try:

"List five supernatural horror story ideas where the monster represents guilt."

Establish the Rules (Then Break Them)

One of the most effective ways to use the supernatural in horror is to establish clear, simple rules—then slowly show how those rules can be bent, broken, or misunderstood.

For example:

- The demon only comes at night... until it doesn't.
- The cursed object only affects the person who touches it... until the curse spreads.
- The ghost can't leave the house... until it follows the protagonist home.

These rule breaks create shock, escalate the stakes, and make the supernatural feel unpredictable.

You can use ChatGPT to quickly draft these rules:

"Create five supernatural rules for a horror story involving a cursed mirror."

Decide How Visible the Supernatural Will Be

Some horror stories make the supernatural **loud and obvious.** You see the ghost. You watch the demon crawl out of the darkness.

Others keep it in the background—unseen, suggested, implied. This can be just as effective (sometimes more) because it plays on the reader's imagination.

The approach you choose will shape the entire tone of your story.

You can ask ChatGPT:

"List five ways to imply supernatural horror without showing the monster."

Use the Supernatural to Isolate the Protagonist

The supernatural is often the thing that separates the protagonist from everyone else. No one believes them. No one else can see it. They're trapped in a nightmare that only they understand.

This is where horror and psychological dread intersect. The supernatural becomes a wedge, driving the protagonist away from safety, sanity, and help.

Control the Reveal

A common mistake horror writers make is revealing the supernatural element too early—or dumping all the information at once. Horror is about tension and mystery. You want to reveal the supernatural **slowly**, scene by scene.

Maybe the protagonist hears whispers at night. Then they see shadows. Then they find an old newspaper article about a tragedy in the house. And only near the climax do they fully understand the supernatural force they're facing.

You can ask ChatGPT to help structure this:

"Outline a horror story where the supernatural threat is revealed gradually over five key scenes."

Make It Personal

The supernatural should tie back to your protagonist. Why is it targeting them? What does it force them to face? How does it reflect their fears, guilt, or flaws?

The scariest monsters aren't the ones lurking in the dark—they're the ones that feel like they know you.

Quick ChatGPT Trick

If you're stuck for ideas, try:

"Describe a terrifying supernatural entity based on the fear of abandonment."

This will give you a monster or force that's tied to real human emotions, making it hit harder.

Supernatural Doesn't Mean Illogical

Even though the supernatural breaks the laws of nature, it should still follow some **internal logic**. Readers will suspend disbelief—but only if your story plays fair. The supernatural force should have rules, limitations, and consequences. Make it clear what it wants, what it can do, and how it can be stopped—or not stopped.

Use the Supernatural to Drive the Story

Finally, the supernatural shouldn't just hover in the background. It should drive the plot forward. Every time the protagonist learns something about the supernatural, the stakes should rise. The horror should get closer. The choices should get harder.

The supernatural element isn't just window dressing—it's the engine of your story's fear.

Writing Psychological Horror That Gets Under the Skin

Some horror stories terrify you with blood and monsters. Others creep into your mind, curl up there, and refuse to leave. That's the magic of **psychological horror.** It doesn't rely on jump scares or gore. It's not about what's hiding in the shadows—it's about what's hiding in your own head. And when you write it well, it's the kind of horror that sticks with your readers long after they've finished the last page.

In this chapter, we're going to talk about how to craft psychological horror that truly gets under the skin—and how you can use ChatGPT to help you pull it off fast, even when you're writing your story in a single day.

What Is Psychological Horror?

Psychological horror is all about **fear of the mind.** It plays with perception, doubt, sanity, and emotional vulnerability. The terror isn't just external—it's internal. Readers don't just fear the monster; they fear what the protagonist is thinking, feeling, or hiding.

Think of stories like *The Shining*, *Black Swan*, *The Babadook*, or *Jacob's Ladder*. The scariest thing isn't the ghost or the killer—it's what's happening inside the protagonist's head.

The Core Ingredients of Psychological Horror

If you want your psychological horror story to hit hard, you need to build it around a few key elements:

1. Unreliable Reality

Your protagonist—and your reader—should never be 100% sure what's real. The world around them should feel unstable.

Are they seeing things? Dreaming? Losing their mind? Being manipulated?

You want the reader to question everything, just like the protagonist.

You can use ChatGPT to help set this up:

"Write a scene where a horror protagonist begins to doubt what's real."

2. Emotional Vulnerability

The best psychological horror stories aren't about external monsters—they're about **internal wounds.** Grief, guilt, trauma, regret, fear of losing control.

The supernatural elements (if any) usually reflect these emotional wounds. The horror is personal.

For example:

- A character haunted by the ghost of someone they couldn't save.
- A protagonist who sees monsters every time they lose control of their anger.
- A cursed house that amplifies the protagonist's depression.

3. Isolation

Psychological horror often isolates the protagonist. No one believes them. No one can help. Sometimes, they even isolate themselves, because they can't trust what's happening in their own mind.

This isolation makes the horror worse—it traps the protagonist with their own thoughts.

4. Doubt and Uncertainty

The more your protagonist doubts themselves, the more the reader doubts everything. Was that shadow a monster—or just a trick of the light? Is the friend trying to help—or hiding something?

You can use ChatGPT to brainstorm these moments fast:

"List five ways to make a psychological horror protagonist doubt their own sanity."

How to Structure Psychological Horror

The key to writing psychological horror is **slow escalation.**

Start with small cracks in reality. A strange noise. A dream that feels too real. A conversation that doesn't make sense.

Then widen those cracks, scene by scene, until the protagonist (and the reader) can't tell what's real anymore.

You can structure this using a simple progression:

1. **Normalcy:** The protagonist's world seems stable.
2. **Disruption:** Small, unsettling events begin.
3. **Unraveling:** The protagonist starts to lose control.
4. **Confrontation:** The protagonist faces their worst fear—internal or external.
5. **Collapse or Clarity:** Either the protagonist loses their mind completely, or they confront the horror and survive—changed forever.

You can ask ChatGPT to help map this out:

"Outline a psychological horror story where the protagonist questions their sanity."

Techniques to Write Psychological Horror Effectively

Here are some quick tricks you can use as you write:

Play with Perception: Describe things vaguely. Let the reader wonder if what's happening is real.

Use Unreliable Narration: Let the protagonist lie to themselves—or the reader.

Show Emotional Reactions: Don't describe the monster—describe how the protagonist feels seeing it. Terror, confusion, dread.

Use Symbols: Recurring images, dreams, or objects that carry emotional weight. A broken mirror. A missing photograph. A shadow that looks familiar.

Create Internal Conflict: The protagonist is fighting not just the horror—but themselves.

Quick ChatGPT Trick

If you need help layering in the psychological tension, try:

"Write an internal monologue for a horror protagonist who's afraid they're losing their mind."

The Payoff

Psychological horror doesn't always end with a big, clear resolution. Sometimes, the scariest thing is what's left unsaid, unresolved.

Maybe the protagonist never knows if the horror was real. Maybe they survive—but can't trust their own mind.

That lingering uncertainty is what makes psychological horror so powerful. It crawls under your skin and stays there.

Why Readers Love Psychological Horror

Because it's not about the monster. It's about the part of themselves they don't want to face.

When you write psychological horror well, you're not just scaring your readers—you're making them question what's real in their own lives.

How to Make the Reader Feel Unsafe

If there's one thing that makes a horror story unforgettable, it's when the reader feels like they're not safe—not on the page, not in their own home, not even in their own head. A good horror story doesn't just scare the reader; it unsettles them, shakes their foundation, makes them check behind the door before they go to bed.

That's the goal: **to make the reader feel unsafe.** And not just once with a jump scare, but all the way through.

In this chapter, we're going to talk about how to do that and how you can use ChatGPT to help you build that creeping, uncomfortable, can't-look-away tension in your horror story—even when you're writing it fast.

Why Feeling Unsafe Matters in Horror

Horror is about stripping away comfort. When readers pick up a horror story, they expect to be scared—but when you can make them feel like nothing is stable, like anything could happen, that's when the story really starts to live inside their heads.

Feeling unsafe is about more than just monsters and violence. It's about making the reader question:

- What's real?
- Who can be trusted?
- Will the protagonist survive?
- Will the horror ever stop?

How to Make the Reader Feel Unsafe

Here are some of the most effective ways to build that feeling:

1. Break the Rules

Readers expect certain things when they open a book. They expect the main character to survive. They expect certain beats and resolutions. In horror, you can—and should—break those rules.

Kill a character the reader thought was safe. Break the "final girl" trope. Let the monster win. Make it clear from the start: **No one is safe.**

You can use ChatGPT to help brainstorm ways to break expectations:

"List five ways to subvert reader expectations in a horror story."

2. Unreliable Perspective

Make the reader question what's real. If your protagonist is doubting their own sanity, the reader will too. If the world around them keeps shifting, readers won't know what to trust.

Play with perception. Describe things vaguely. Let the reader wonder if what they're seeing is true—or a trick.

3. Atmosphere and Setting

Use setting to make the reader uneasy. Empty streets. Abandoned buildings. Flickering lights. Sounds that don't have a source.

Every scene should make the reader feel like something is off. Like the world itself is dangerous.

You can ask ChatGPT:

"Describe a horror setting that makes the reader feel unsafe."

4. Sensory Details That Disorient

Use sensory detail to unsettle the reader. Let them feel the sticky sweat of fear, hear the faint scratching at the window, smell the rot in the air.

The more vivid the details, the more real the fear feels.

5. Threats From Every Direction

Don't let the horror come from just one place. Create danger from the environment, from other characters, from the protagonist's own mind.

The reader should feel like there's **no way out.**

You can use ChatGPT to brainstorm:

"List five ways to make the protagonist feel surrounded by danger in a horror story."

6. Take Away Control

One of the fastest ways to make a reader feel unsafe is to take control away from the protagonist. Trap them. Disorient them. Let them lose time, memory, or autonomy.

If the protagonist has no control, the reader feels powerless too.

7. End Scenes on Uncertainty

Never end a scene neatly. Leave the reader with a question, a threat, or a cliffhanger. Make them turn the page because they need to know if the protagonist survives—but make them dread finding out.

You can use ChatGPT to help craft these endings:

"Write five horror scene endings that leave the reader feeling unsafe."

8. Blur the Line between Reality and Nightmare

The best horror stories make readers wonder if the nightmare could be real. Use everyday fears—losing a loved one, being watched, losing control—and mix them with the supernatural.

When readers start to see the horror in their own lives, they'll feel unsafe even after they've put the book down.

Why This Works

Making the reader feel unsafe isn't about jump scares or gore. It's about **unsettling them emotionally and psychologically.** When they can't trust the world you've created—or the characters in it—they'll lean forward, tense, unable to stop reading.

Quick ChatGPT Trick

When you're writing and want to amp up the tension, ask:

"How can I make this horror scene feel more unsafe for the reader?"

You'll get instant suggestions to ratchet up the fear.

Remember:

You're not just telling a scary story. You're creating an experience. You want the reader to feel like they're trapped in the dark with the protagonist, no flashlight, no exit.

The Role of Sound, Smell, and Senses in Horror Writing

When people think of horror stories, they often picture creepy settings, terrifying monsters, and shocking deaths—but what really makes a horror story feel alive and inescapable is how you **use the senses.** Not just what your characters see, but what they **hear, smell, touch, and even taste.** The senses are how we experience the world, so when you tap into them, you make the reader feel like they're right there in the nightmare.

In this chapter, we're going to talk about how to use sound, smell, and the full range of sensory detail to crank up the fear—and how you can use ChatGPT to generate these details fast when you're writing your horror story in one day.

Why Sensory Detail Matters in Horror

Horror is about atmosphere. It's about making the reader feel trapped in a place that's hostile, threatening, and full of dread. And nothing builds atmosphere like sensory details.

The human brain is wired to react to certain sounds, smells, and sensations. When you describe these vividly, you bypass the reader's logic and hit them right in the gut. Their heart rate spikes. Their stomach churns. They feel the fear, even if they know it's fiction.

The Power of Sound

Sound is one of the most effective tools in horror because it can't be escaped. You can close your eyes—but you can't stop hearing things.

Use sound to signal danger, build tension, or hint at something lurking out of sight. Think of:

- A faint scratching at the window.
- The drip-drip-drip of water echoing in a dark hallway.
- A voice whispering the protagonist's name when no one is there.
- Heavy breathing coming from behind a door.

You can use ChatGPT to help you quickly brainstorm creepy sounds:

"List ten creepy sounds to use in a horror story."

Also, think about how your protagonist **reacts** to the sounds. Do they freeze? Do they try to explain it away? Do they plug their ears to block it out, only to hear it inside their own head?

The Power of Smell

Smell is the most **primal** of the senses. It's directly linked to memory and emotion. A single smell can bring back trauma, trigger nausea, or make a character's skin crawl.

In horror, smell is your secret weapon. It's often overlooked—but when used right, it can make a scene unforgettable.

Examples:

- The sickly sweet smell of decay in an empty house.
- The sharp scent of iron and blood.

- The stink of mildew, mold, or something rotting in the walls.
- The smell of smoke, hinting at a fire long extinguished.
- The faint smell of perfume in a room that's supposed to be empty.

You can ask ChatGPT:

"Describe the smell of an abandoned asylum in a horror story."

The Power of Touch and Physical Sensation

Don't forget the physical sensations of fear and dread. Describe how the world feels against the protagonist's skin. The cold air. The sticky sweat. The crawling sensation on the back of their neck.

Also, describe how the environment interacts with them:

- The rough texture of peeling wallpaper under their fingers.
- The wet squelch of mud—or something worse—underfoot.
- The sudden, sharp pain when something unseen brushes past them.

These details make the reader feel like they're **inside the scene,** not just watching from a distance.

Layering the Senses Together

The real magic happens when you combine multiple senses. For example:

"The hallway stretched into darkness, the air heavy with the smell of damp wood and something sour. Every step echoed too loud, the creak of the floorboards slicing through the silence like a scream."

By layering smell, sound, and physical sensation, you create a full-body experience.

You can use ChatGPT to help you layer sensory detail fast:

"Write a horror scene description using sound, smell, and touch."

Don't Overload the Reader

It's easy to get carried away with sensory detail. But too much will bog down your story and slow the pacing. Think of sensory detail like seasoning. Sprinkle it throughout your scenes—but don't drown your reader in adjectives.

The goal is to make them feel the atmosphere without pulling them out of the story.

How to Use Sensory Detail Strategically

Use sensory detail when you want to:

- Build tension before a big scare.
- Make a quiet scene unsettling.
- Signal danger before the protagonist knows it's there.
- Pull the reader deeper into the protagonist's experience.

And remember—you don't need to describe everything. Pick the detail that matters most. Sometimes, a single sound or smell can carry an entire scene.

Quick ChatGPT Trick

If you're writing a scene and it feels flat, try asking:

"What sensory details can I add to make this horror scene more immersive?"

You'll get instant suggestions you can plug into your draft.

Why This Works

Readers come to horror for the experience. They want to feel the dread, the fear, the panic. When you use sound, smell, and physical sensations effectively, you're not just telling them a story—you're dragging them into it.

You want them to hear the footsteps behind them. Smell the decay in the air. Feel the cold breath on the back of their neck.

Red Herrings and Misdirection in Horror Plots

If you want to keep your readers on edge, unsure of what's coming next, and constantly second-guessing what they think they know—you need to master the art of **red herrings and misdirection.** These two storytelling tools aren't just for mystery novels; they're essential ingredients in a gripping horror plot.

Horror isn't just about showing the monster—it's about what's lurking in the shadows, what's almost revealed but not quite, and what's hiding behind every turn. Readers should feel like they're trying to put together a puzzle, only to realize the pieces don't fit the way they thought.

In this chapter, we'll break down how to use red herrings and misdirection effectively, without annoying your readers or confusing your plot. And, of course, how to use ChatGPT to whip up these tricks quickly when you're writing your horror story in one day.

What Is a Red Herring?

A red herring is a false clue. It's something that looks important but isn't. It leads the reader (and sometimes the characters) down the wrong path, making them believe the threat is coming from one direction—only for it to strike from somewhere else.

In horror, red herrings are incredibly useful because they keep the tension alive. If the reader thinks they've figured out the mystery too soon, the fear evaporates. But if you keep them guessing, they stay on edge.

What Is Misdirection?

Misdirection is broader than a red herring. It's about **controlling the reader's attention.** Making them look one way while the danger is creeping up from another direction.

Think of it like a magician's trick. You show them one hand, while the real trick is happening with the other.

How to Use Red Herrings in Horror

The best red herrings in horror serve two purposes:

1. They add tension and suspicion.
2. They reveal something about the characters or world, even if they're false leads.

For example:

- The creepy neighbor who seems suspicious—but is actually harmless.
- Strange noises in the attic—turns out to be rats, but the real horror is in the basement.
- A friend who disappears, leading the protagonist to think they're dead—but they're actually the villain.

You can ask ChatGPT to help you brainstorm red herrings:

"List five red herring characters or clues for a haunted house horror story."

How to Use Misdirection in Horror

Misdirection is about where you shine the spotlight. You can:

- Build tension around one threat, while hiding the real danger.
- Make readers focus on the external horror, while the true threat is psychological.
- Distract readers with gore or violence, while the real horror is something quieter, creepier.

The key to good misdirection is to make it **fair.** You can trick your reader, but you can't cheat them. When they look back, the clues should have been there all along.

How to Plan Red Herrings and Misdirection Fast

Since you're writing your horror story in a day, you don't have time to overthink this. So here's a simple strategy:

1. **List the true source of horror.**
   What's the real threat in your story? A ghost? A murderer? A curse?
2. **Brainstorm three to five false threats.**
   These are the red herrings. Creepy but harmless characters. Misleading clues. Dead ends.
3. **Map out where to reveal each one.**
   Drop these false leads at key points to keep the reader guessing.

You can ask ChatGPT to help with this quickly:

"Outline five moments of misdirection in a horror story about a haunted hotel."

Balance is Key

You don't want your story to be one big fake-out. Red herrings and misdirection are seasoning, not the whole meal. Too many false leads, and readers will get frustrated or stop trusting you.

Use them to **enhance** the mystery and tension, not to stall the plot.

How to Make Red Herrings Work Emotionally

The best red herrings aren't random—they reveal something about the characters or world. Maybe the creepy neighbor isn't the villain—but they're hiding something else. Maybe the weird noises aren't supernatural—but they expose the protagonist's paranoia.

Even false leads can deepen your characters and theme.

Use Misdirection in Scene Structure

You can also use misdirection at the scene level. For example:

- Start a scene with a jump scare that turns out to be harmless—only to follow it with real danger.
- Distract the protagonist (and reader) with a loud, violent event—while something terrifying happens quietly in the background.

Quick ChatGPT Trick

If you need fresh ideas, try:

"Give me five misdirection ideas for a horror story climax."

You'll get fast, usable options to keep readers guessing until the very end.

Why This Works

Horror is about uncertainty. When readers don't know what's coming, when they can't trust what they're seeing, when every clue could be a trap—they're scared. Red herrings and misdirection feed that uncertainty.

You want your readers constantly asking:

- Is this the real threat?
- Can I trust this character?
- Is the horror what I think it is?

And when you finally reveal the truth—you want them to gasp, flip back through the pages, and realize the clues were there all along.

Writing About Fear of the Unknown

If there's one fear that fuels almost every great horror story, it's the **fear of the unknown.** You can throw all the gore, monsters, and jump scares you want into a horror plot—but the thing that truly gets under people's skin is what they **don't know.** What they can't see. What they can't explain. What's just outside the flashlight's beam.

In this chapter, we're going to dive into why the unknown is the backbone of horror storytelling, how to use it to terrify your readers, and how you can get ChatGPT to help you harness this primal fear quickly when you're writing your horror story in one day.

Why Fear of the Unknown Works

People fear what they don't understand. It's wired into our survival instincts. In the real world, we're scared of the dark, of strange noises, of being alone in an unfamiliar place—not because of what's actually there, but because we **don't know** what might be there.

That's why the scariest moments in horror are often not when the monster shows up, but in the **silence before.** The empty hallway. The closed door. The unanswered question.

The Unknown in Storytelling

The fear of the unknown shows up in many ways in horror stories:

- **Mysterious monsters or entities:** Creatures you never fully see or understand.
- **Unanswered questions:** What happened here? Why is this place cursed?
- **Blurred reality:** Is this really happening, or is it in the protagonist's head?
- **Unpredictable outcomes:** Who will survive? Will anyone?

You can use ChatGPT to help brainstorm these unknowns fast:

"List five unknown elements that could terrify readers in a horror story."

How to Use the Unknown in Your Plot

When you're writing your horror story, structure your plot around the **absence of answers.** Every time your protagonist learns something, it should raise more questions. Every discovery should make things worse.

For example:

- They find an old journal—but it's missing the last pages.
- They learn the monster's name—but not what it wants.
- They escape the haunted house—but something follows them.

You want the reader to feel like they're descending deeper and deeper into a darkness that has no bottom.

The Unknown in Characters

Characters can also embody the fear of the unknown:

- The creepy neighbor who knows more than they're saying.
- The missing family member whose disappearance is never fully explained.
- The protagonist themselves, who doesn't remember what they've done.

When your characters hide secrets, the reader feels unsafe—because they don't know who to trust.

You can use ChatGPT to quickly generate these character mysteries:

"List five horror character backstories filled with unknown secrets."

The Unknown in Setting

Your setting can amplify this fear. Think abandoned towns, dark forests, empty buildings with locked doors and long-forgotten histories. Readers fear these places not because of what's there—but because they don't know what's waiting in the dark.

You can even make everyday places feel unknown. A hospital at night. A motel in the middle of nowhere. A quiet suburban street where something feels just a little off.

How to Keep the Reader in the Dark

Here's the trick to writing fear of the unknown: **Don't show everything.**

The worst thing you can do is explain too much too soon. Keep your horror vague and creeping. Let readers fill in the blanks with their own fears.

For example: Instead of:

"The monster stood ten feet tall, with yellow eyes and sharp claws."

Try:

"Something moved in the shadows, its shape shifting and stretching where it shouldn't."

The less you describe, the more the reader's imagination runs wild.

Pacing the Unknown

The fear of the unknown works best when it's slow and steady. Let the mystery build, layer by layer. Keep your reader—and your protagonist—off balance.

A good structure to follow:

1. **Establish the unknown.**
   Hint at something wrong without revealing anything.
2. **Raise questions.**

Every discovery leads to more mysteries.
3. **Tease answers.**
Offer clues—but never enough.
4. **Reveal—but not everything.**
Even at the end, leave something unanswered.

You can ask ChatGPT to help structure this:

"Outline a horror story that centers on fear of the unknown."

Why This Works

The human mind is a horror machine. When you leave gaps in your story—questions unanswered, shadows unexplained—readers fill those gaps with their **own fears.** And nothing you could write will ever be scarier than what the reader imagines in the dark.

Quick ChatGPT Trick

If you want to amp up the unknown in a scene, try:

"Write a horror scene where the protagonist can't see or explain what's stalking them."

Leave Some Questions Unanswered

The best horror stories don't tie up every loose end. When the last page turns, readers should still be wondering:

- What was really going on?
- Was the protagonist crazy?
- Is the horror really over?

That lingering uncertainty is what makes the story stick with them long after they've finished reading.

How to Use ChatGPT to Punch Up Scary Dialogue

There's something special about horror dialogue. It's not just what your characters say—it's what's **between the lines.** The whispers, the panic, the lies, the dread. Great horror dialogue isn't polite or pretty. It's raw. It's desperate. It makes the reader's skin crawl because of what's being said—or what isn't being said.

But let's be honest: writing truly chilling dialogue can be hard, especially when you're trying to write your entire horror story in a single day. That's why you've got ChatGPT in your corner. Not just to crank out ideas and descriptions, but to help you **punch up your scary dialogue fast and effectively.**

In this chapter, I'm going to show you exactly how to do it.

What Makes Horror Dialogue Scary

Good horror dialogue isn't about long speeches. It's about tension, fear, lies, and the cracks in what characters say. It's about what's hiding behind their words.

Here's what makes horror dialogue work:

- **Panic and fear:** Short, clipped sentences. Repetition. Characters cutting each other off.
- **Denial:** Characters trying to explain things away, even as the horror closes in.
- **Foreboding:** Cryptic warnings. Half-told stories. Whispers of what's to come.
- **Emotional breakdowns:** Screaming. Crying. Silence.
- **False calm:** Characters pretending everything's fine when it's clearly not.

You want your dialogue to drip with tension, so the reader feels like every conversation is about to explode.

How ChatGPT Can Help

You can use ChatGPT to generate, rewrite, and sharpen dialogue fast. Here's how:

1. Generate First Draft Dialogue

When you're writing quickly, you don't have time to labor over every line. So use ChatGPT to spit out raw dialogue you can shape.

Prompt example:

"Write a creepy conversation between two characters in a haunted house."

You'll get something rough and ready that you can tweak or drop straight into your story.

2. Add Subtext

Horror dialogue is powerful when it has subtext—when characters are saying one thing but meaning another.

Prompt example:

"Rewrite this conversation so the characters are scared but pretending not to be."

ChatGPT can instantly give you dialogue filled with tension and double meaning.

3. Make Dialogue Shorter and Snappier

In horror, less is often more. Long speeches kill tension. Short, sharp lines keep the reader's pulse racing.

Prompt example:

"Rewrite this horror dialogue to make it shorter and more tense."

You can even use ChatGPT to trim bloated dialogue scenes while keeping the fear intact.

4. Add Personality and Voice

Good dialogue reflects character. A scared teenager doesn't talk like a grizzled detective. A mother protecting her child won't speak like a college professor.

Prompt example:

"Rewrite this dialogue so the protagonist sounds terrified but determined."

You can fine-tune how each character sounds without spending hours fussing over it.

5. Inject Foreboding or Cryptic Warnings

Sometimes you want a character to say something ominous without explaining it outright. Something that makes the reader's stomach drop.

Prompt example:

"Write a cryptic, creepy warning from an old man in a horror story."

These little lines can give your story texture and tension.

Techniques to Keep Dialogue Scary

Here are a few simple tricks you can use (and ask ChatGPT to help you with):

Use Silence: Sometimes the scariest line is the one that isn't said. A character trailing off. A pause. A character staring instead of answering.

Echo and Repetition:

"Did you hear that?"

"Hear what?"

"That... tapping. It's getting closer."

Repetition creates rhythm and tension.

Questions with No Answers:

Characters asking questions and getting silence, evasion, or lies is unsettling.

Sudden Changes in Tone:

A character laughing when they should be crying. A whisper turning into a scream.

How to Use ChatGPT on the Fly

When you're in writing mode and you hit a dialogue scene that's falling flat, don't stop and overthink. Just type:

"Write a tense, creepy dialogue exchange for this scene [insert brief description]."

You can also keep a running list of scary lines, cryptic warnings, or terrified outbursts. Any time you need a punchy line, grab one.

Examples

Here's how you can use ChatGPT quickly:

Your Prompt:

"Two characters trapped in a haunted hospital. One hears something. Write tense dialogue."

ChatGPT Might Give You:

"Did you hear that?"

"No. What?"

"A voice. Down the hall."

"You're hearing things."

"No, it said my name."

"Don't. Just... don't."

You can tighten, tweak, and drop it straight into your draft.

Why Dialogue Matters in Horror

Dialogue isn't filler. It's not just there to move the plot. In horror, dialogue is one of your sharpest tools to build tension, reveal character, and make the reader feel unsafe.

When characters whisper, scream, deny, or break down, the reader feels it.

Quick ChatGPT Trick

If you want to build a tense dialogue scene fast, try:

"Write a short dialogue scene where two characters argue about whether the monster is real."

Then tweak it for your characters and plot.

Final Thought

When you're writing your horror story in one day, you don't have time to craft every line perfectly. That's fine. Get ChatGPT to help you draft and refine your scary dialogue fast—so you can focus on keeping the tension high and the story moving.

How to Make Your Characters' Decisions Terrifying

One of the things that separates a mediocre horror story from a great one isn't just the monster, or the setting, or the gore—it's the **choices the characters make.** If you want your horror story to grab readers by the throat, you've got to make your characters' decisions terrifying. Not because they're stupid decisions (although sometimes they can be), but because they're desperate, dangerous, morally questionable, or emotionally devastating.

In this chapter, we're going to break down how to make your characters' choices terrifying—both for them and for the reader—and how you can use ChatGPT to help shape these decisions fast, even when you're writing your horror story in a single day.

Why Decisions Matter in Horror

In horror, the scariest thing isn't always the monster—it's what the characters do when the monster shows up. Readers want to see characters struggle, panic, make mistakes, and face impossible choices. That's what keeps them hooked. That's what makes the story unpredictable and emotionally charged.

Terrifying decisions force your characters to:

- Face their fears
- Sacrifice something important
- Choose between bad and worse
- Cross moral lines
- Risk everything

And every time they make a decision, the consequences should make things worse.

How to Make Decisions Terrifying

Here's how you can structure horrifying choices into your story:

1. No Good Options

The best horror decisions happen when the protagonist is trapped between two terrible outcomes.

Save a friend or save themselves. Open the door or run the other way. Tell the truth or hide the secret.

Make sure every major decision costs something.

You can use ChatGPT to help brainstorm these choices:

"List five terrifying choices a protagonist could face in a horror story."

2. Force the Character to Act Under Pressure

Give your characters no time to think. The monster is right behind them. The ghost is whispering in their ear. Their flashlight is dying.

Decisions made in panic are messy and dangerous—and that's what makes them terrifying.

3. Make the Reader Yell at the Page

One of the great joys of reading (or watching) horror is screaming at the characters:

"No! Don't go in there!"

Lean into this. Give your characters moments when they choose to do something risky, reckless, or emotionally driven—even if it's the wrong choice.

4. Tie Decisions to Character Flaws

A decision is scarier when it's personal. Make sure your characters' flaws and fears drive their choices.

For example:

- A character who can't let go of the past decides to investigate the haunted house.
- A character who feels responsible for others sacrifices themselves.
- A character who's terrified of being alone chooses to trust the wrong person.

You can use ChatGPT to help connect character flaws to story decisions:

"List five horror story character flaws that lead to bad decisions."

5. Moral Dilemmas Make It Worse

The most chilling decisions are the ones that challenge the character's morals. Would they kill to survive? Would they sacrifice someone they love? Would they let an innocent person die?

Horror is the perfect genre to explore what people will do when everything is on the line.

You can ask ChatGPT:

"List five moral dilemmas a protagonist could face in a horror story."

How to Structure Terrifying Decisions in Your Story

When you're writing your outline (which we'll cover again soon), map out the major decision points.

For each one, ask:

- What are the options?
- What will the protagonist lose no matter what?
- How will this choice escalate the horror?

Then, make sure each decision leaves the protagonist worse off, not better.

Quick ChatGPT Trick

When you're drafting a scene and want to amp up the tension, try:

"What terrifying decision could the protagonist face in this scene?"

You'll get quick, usable ideas you can drop straight into your story.

Why This Works

When your characters are forced to make impossible choices, readers feel the tension. They're not just watching the horror unfold—they're emotionally invested in what the protagonist will do next. Every decision becomes a source of dread.

And when the protagonist's choices lead to consequences, the reader feels trapped right alongside them.

Keep the Pressure On

Terrifying decisions don't just belong at the climax. Scatter them throughout your story. Every act should force the protagonist to make a choice that costs them something. By the end, they should be broken, bleeding, and changed forever by the choices they've made.

Final Thought

The scariest thing in horror isn't the monster. It's watching a character you care about make the wrong choice—and knowing they'll have to live (or die) with it.

Writing the Horror Story You Want to Read

If you've made it this far, you've learned how to build tension, craft terrifying characters, use sensory horror, misdirect readers, and crank out dialogue that drips with dread. But now, here's the real secret to writing a gripping, scary, unforgettable horror story in one day: **write the horror story you want to read.**

That sounds simple, but it's the step most writers forget. Too often, writers chase trends, copy what's popular, or try to engineer scares based on what they think readers want. But horror hits hardest when it's personal—when it comes from your own fears, fascinations, and dark imagination.

In this chapter, we're going to talk about how to tap into the horror that thrills you, and how you can use ChatGPT to help you bring that vision to life quickly and effectively.

What Scares You?

Before you can write a story that scares others, you need to ask yourself:

What scares me?

It could be:

- Losing control
- Being alone
- Dying in the dark
- Someone you love turning against you
- The unknown
- The supernatural
- Psychological breakdown

Your fear is your fuel. When you write a horror story that taps into what genuinely unsettles you, that authenticity bleeds through the page. Readers can tell when a writer is just going through the motions—and when a writer is pouring their own dread into the story.

Take a minute and write down the three things that terrify you the most.

If you're stuck, ask ChatGPT:

"List twenty common human fears I could use in a horror story."

Then circle the ones that hit you hardest.

The Horror You Love

Think about the horror stories, movies, and games that have stayed with you. What do they have in common? Is it the atmosphere? The monster? The psychological unraveling? The twist ending?

You're not writing this story to win awards. You're writing the story that would keep **you** up at night.

If you love creepy ghost stories—write one.

If you love survival horror—write one.

If you love slow-burn psychological horror that never explains everything—write that.

What Kind of Horror Experience Do You Want to Create?

Not all horror is created equal. Before you start writing, decide what kind of experience you want the reader to have:

- Do you want them to be terrified and tense the whole time?
- Do you want to slowly creep them out and leave them unsettled at the end?
- Do you want to make them squirm with gore?
- Do you want them to question their own reality?

When you know what kind of horror **you** want to experience, you can shape your story around it.

You can ask ChatGPT:

"List five different horror story moods and how to create them."

Inject Your Voice

There's no rulebook for horror. You don't have to copy Stephen King, Shirley Jackson, or Junji Ito. You can write in your own voice—whether that's gritty, poetic, blunt, darkly funny, or dreamlike.

Your story will be scarier if it feels like it's coming from **you,** not from a formula.

Write the Horror You Haven't Seen Yet

We've all read stories about haunted houses, serial killers, and possessed dolls. If there's a type of horror story you wish existed but haven't seen—**write it.**

Blend genres. Flip tropes. Break rules.

Maybe you want to write a haunted house story where the house isn't haunted—the protagonist is.

Maybe you want to write a slasher where the killer is a supernatural force no one can see.

Maybe you want to write a horror story with a happy ending, or one where the monster wins.

Whatever you're itching to read but can't find—that's the story you should write.

You can use ChatGPT to help you get creative fast:

"Give me five fresh horror story concepts that haven't been done before."

Don't Worry About What's "Good"

When you're writing fast—especially in one day—it's easy to get caught up worrying about whether your story is "good enough." Forget that. Your first goal is to write a horror story that **you** would want to read.

If it creeps you out, shocks you, or leaves you smiling at how dark it gets—you're doing it right.

You can always edit later. But if you're not excited, scared, or unsettled by what you're writing, the reader won't be either.

How ChatGPT Can Help You Write the Story You Want to Read

You don't have to build this story alone. Use ChatGPT to:

- Generate fresh story ideas that fit your specific fears and tastes.
- Help you plot twists you would love as a reader.
- Punch up dialogue in your style.
- Describe creepy settings the way you like them.
- Brainstorm unique monsters or supernatural elements that scare you.

You can even type:

"Help me write a horror story that includes [insert your favorite horror themes]."

ChatGPT will never replace your voice—but it can speed up the process and help you write a horror story that feels like something only **you** could have written.

Final Thought

Horror is one of the most personal genres out there. It's about fear, survival, death, and the unknown. The stories that stick with readers aren't the ones that follow a perfect formula—they're the ones that feel like the writer cracked open their own nightmares and spilled them onto the page.

So as you prepare to write your story in one day, stop worrying about the rules. Write the horror story you want to read. Make yourself uncomfortable. Make yourself afraid. Because if you're scared—the reader will be too.

Avoiding Horror Clichés and Making Them Fresh

Every horror fan knows the clichés. The creepy doll. The group splitting up. The car that won't start. The protagonist who runs upstairs instead of out the front door. You've seen them, I've seen them, readers have seen them—and when they show up lazily in a story, they kill the tension faster than a chainsaw through butter.

But here's the thing: clichés exist because they **work.** They're tropes that, at some point, scared the hell out of people. The problem isn't the cliché itself—it's when it's predictable, lazy, and used without any fresh spin. Your job as a horror writer is to either **avoid** these clichés altogether or **twist them into something new** so your readers don't roll their eyes—they grip the edge of their seat.

In this chapter, we're going to talk about how to recognize horror clichés, how to dodge them, and how to make them fresh if you decide to use them. Plus, how to get ChatGPT to help you with this fast while you're writing your horror story in one day.

Common Horror Clichés

Let's start by calling them out. Here are some of the biggest offenders:

- The group splitting up ("We'll cover more ground!")
- The car that won't start just when the monster is near
- The haunted house built on a burial ground
- The protagonist investigating a noise instead of running
- The final girl trope
- The phone dying when they need help
- The monster that can only be killed in one specific, overly complex way
- The old person who knows the dark secret but won't explain it clearly

Readers have seen these a thousand times. If you use them exactly as they are, your story will feel tired.

How to Avoid Horror Clichés

The simplest way to avoid clichés is to **make different choices.** If you see your character heading toward a cliché moment, stop and ask:

- What would a real person do here?
- How can I surprise the reader?
- What's the opposite of what usually happens?

For example:

- Instead of the group splitting up, have them stay together—and the horror picks them off anyway.
- Instead of the car not starting, maybe it starts, but the protagonist is too scared or injured to drive.
- Instead of a haunted house, maybe it's a brand-new, high-tech house with something evil inside.

You can ask ChatGPT to help flip clichés quickly:

"List ten common horror clichés and suggest fresh ways to twist each one."

How to Make Clichés Fresh

Sometimes, you might **want** to use a cliché—but with a twist that makes it feel new. Here's how:

1. Subvert Expectations

Set up the cliché, then pull the rug out.

The reader thinks the protagonist is about to run upstairs—but they calmly walk out the front door... only to find the real horror is outside.

2. Make It Self-Aware

Characters can call out clichés in dialogue. This can add humor and tension. *"We're not splitting up. That's how people die in horror movies."*

And then, something forces them apart anyway.

3. Add Complexity

Instead of the old man who warns the protagonist but speaks in riddles, maybe he's the one who started the curse. Maybe he's lying.

4. Change the Setting

A haunted house is a cliché. But what about a haunted **shopping mall**? Or an abandoned **space station**? A cursed **smartphone app**?

You can use ChatGPT to quickly brainstorm fresh settings:

"Give me five unique settings for a horror story that avoid clichés."

5. Give the Protagonist Agency

One of the biggest clichés in horror is characters making dumb choices just to move the plot. Instead, write smart characters who do everything right—and still lose. That's terrifying.

Using ChatGPT to Catch and Fix Clichés Fast

When you're writing your horror story quickly, you might accidentally slip into cliché territory. That's fine. You can use ChatGPT to spot and fix them.

Try prompts like: **"Read this scene and tell me if it contains any horror clichés."** or **"Suggest ways to rewrite this horror scene to avoid common tropes."**

ChatGPT can act as your horror editor on the fly, pointing out when you're falling into predictable patterns.

Why Readers Hate Lazy Clichés

When readers spot a cliché, it breaks the spell. They're no longer in your story—they're thinking about all the other times they've seen that same thing. It pulls them out of the experience.

But when you twist a cliché, subvert it, or give it a fresh coat of paint, readers love it. They think they know what's coming—and then you surprise them.

Quick ChatGPT Trick

If you're stuck writing a scene and afraid it feels cliché, type:

"What's an unexpected way to write this horror scene so it avoids clichés?"

You'll get fast, creative suggestions to keep your story fresh.

Final Thought

Clichés aren't evil. They're just overused. Your job as a horror writer is to recognize when you're about to lean on one—and either avoid it or twist it into something terrifying and new.

Because horror is about the unknown, the unexpected, the thing you never saw coming. And nothing kills horror faster than predictability.

How to Write an Opening Sentence That Screams Horror

If there's one thing that will make or break your horror story—especially when you're writing fast and need to hook your reader immediately—it's the **opening sentence.** That very first line is your chance to grab the reader by the throat and whisper, *You're not safe here.* A killer first sentence sets the mood, introduces dread, and makes the reader want to know what's lurking in the shadows.

You don't need to overthink it, but you do need to make sure your opening sentence has one job: **pull the reader straight into the nightmare.**

In this chapter, we're going to break down how to craft an opening line that screams horror—and how you can use ChatGPT to help you do it quickly and effectively.

Why the First Sentence Matters in Horror

In most genres, you have a paragraph or two to ease the reader in. In horror? You don't get that luxury. You want to plant a seed of unease immediately. Your reader should feel, right from the start, that something is wrong.

That first line is your chance to:

- Set the tone
- Establish tension
- Tease the mystery
- Deliver a jolt
- Create immediate questions

And since you're writing your horror story in one day, you need that sentence to do a lot of heavy lifting fast.

What Makes a Great Horror Opening Sentence

Let's break it down. A great horror opening sentence usually has one or more of these elements:

1. A Disturbing Image

Start with something unsettling, grotesque, or strange. *"The thing in the corner wasn't breathing—but it was watching."*

2. A Mystery or Question

Make the reader wonder what's happening right away. *"When I woke up, the walls were bleeding."*

3. A Direct Threat

Start in the middle of the horror. *"They were already inside the house when she locked the door."*

4. A Hint of Something Wrong

A quiet, creepy detail that makes the reader uneasy. *"The town's lights flickered every night at midnight, but no one ever spoke about why."*

5. Emotional Panic or Dread

Open with fear or despair. *"I knew I wouldn't survive the night when the whispers started."*

Quick ChatGPT Trick

When you're ready to write your story and need a strong first line fast, just ask:

"Write five opening sentences for a horror story that immediately create tension and fear."

You'll get options you can use, tweak, or combine to fit your story.

Tailor the Sentence to Your Story

Your first sentence should also match the type of horror story you're writing.

If it's psychological horror, make it unsettling.

If it's survival horror, start with panic.

If it's supernatural horror, hint at the impossible.

For example: **Psychological:**

"The mirror had stopped reflecting her face weeks ago."

Supernatural:

"Every night at three a.m., something knocks on my window from the inside."

Survival:

"The storm had buried the town—and something was moving under the snow."

Common Mistakes to Avoid

When writing a horror opening sentence, watch out for:

- **Over-explaining:** Don't try to tell the whole backstory in one sentence.
- **Generic statements:** Avoid something bland like *"It was a dark and stormy night."*
- **Too much action:** You want tension, not chaos, in the first line.

Use Sensory Detail

If you can, slip in a sensory detail—something the character sees, hears, smells, or feels. That pulls the reader in immediately.

"The smell of burnt hair still clung to the air when they found the first body."

Practice Makes Perfect

One fun way to get good at horror opening lines is to write ten of them in five minutes. Don't overthink—just go for creepy, unsettling, weird. You can even use ChatGPT to help you brainstorm:

"Write ten short, scary first sentences for a horror story."

You'll end up with a list you can use not just for this story, but for future ones too.

Why This Works

A strong opening line is like the first knock at the door in the middle of the night. It doesn't give you all the answers—it makes you want to find out what's on the other side.

When you nail that first sentence, your reader will lean in. Their pulse will quicken. They'll keep reading, because you've promised them one thing: **Something bad is about to happen.**

Final Thought

Don't stress too much about writing the "perfect" first line. Write one that excites you, that feels like a door cracking open to something dark and terrible. You can always tweak it later. But once you've got that sentence down, you've broken the blank page—and that's the hardest part.

Using Dreams and Nightmares in Horror

There's something uniquely terrifying about a nightmare. It's not just that you're powerless or trapped—it's that you can't trust what's real. Your heart's pounding, your skin's clammy, you're running from something that isn't there—and when you wake up, the fear doesn't always go away.

That's why dreams and nightmares are one of horror's oldest and sharpest tools. They blur the line between reality and imagination, between the safe and the unsafe. Used well, they can deepen your story, heighten the tension, and keep readers guessing.

In this chapter, you'll learn how to use dreams and nightmares effectively in your horror story—and how to use ChatGPT to help you write them quickly, even when you're crafting your entire narrative in a single day.

Why Dreams and Nightmares Work in Horror

Dreams are fertile ground for horror because they don't follow the rules. Anything can happen. Logic breaks down. Nightmares tap into **primal, subconscious fear**—the kind you can't explain or escape.

They also serve a few key purposes in horror:

- **Reveal a character's inner fears or trauma**
- **Foreshadow future events**
- **Distort reality so the reader doesn't know what's real**
- **Deliver surreal, terrifying imagery that couldn't exist in the waking world**

Nightmares are like free permission to break every storytelling rule—**if you use them carefully.**

How to Use Nightmares in Your Horror Story

Here's how to use nightmares effectively, without falling into cliché territory:

1. Make Them Personal

Your protagonist's nightmares should reflect their specific fears, regrets, or trauma. If their backstory involves losing a sibling, maybe their nightmares show distorted versions of that loss. If they're terrified of losing control, the nightmare should show them powerless.

You can use ChatGPT to brainstorm:

"Write a nightmare scene for a horror protagonist who feels guilty about a past mistake."

2. Blur the Line Between Dream and Reality

One of the best ways to keep your reader on edge is to make them (and the protagonist) question what's real. Start a scene like it's normal—then twist it until it's clear they're dreaming. Or worse, end a nightmare sequence without letting the protagonist (or the reader) know if they've really woken up.

A reader who can't tell what's real is a reader who stays scared.

3. Use Nightmares for Foreshadowing

Nightmares are a great place to hint at what's coming. You can show images, symbols, or events that won't make sense until later in the story. That keeps readers guessing and builds tension.

For example:

- A nightmare of drowning... and later, the protagonist is trapped in a flooding basement.
- A recurring dream of a door... and at the climax, they find that exact door.

You can use ChatGPT to help build these connections:

"Write a nightmare scene that foreshadows a haunted house's dark secret."

4. Don't Overuse Them

A dream sequence loses its power if you use it too often. If every scare is "just a dream," readers will stop trusting the tension. Use nightmares strategically—when you want to reveal something, shake the protagonist, or crank up the psychological horror.

5. Make the Imagery Disturbing

The beauty of nightmares is that you can go wild. Logic doesn't apply. Time, space, and physics can break down. People can change faces. Shadows can move wrong. The walls can breathe. The world can collapse.

The weirder and more unsettling, the better.

Ask ChatGPT to help you brainstorm:

"Describe five disturbing nightmare images for a horror story."

6. Tie Nightmares to the Plot

A nightmare isn't just filler. It should move the story forward. Maybe it reveals something the protagonist needs to know. Maybe it forces them to face a fear they've been avoiding. Maybe it hints at the horror hunting them.

Common Mistakes to Avoid

There are a few traps you want to avoid when writing nightmare sequences:

- **Making them too long.** A nightmare that drags on will kill the tension.
- **Ending with a cheap "It was just a dream" moment.** Readers hate this unless it actually adds to the story.
- **Using generic dream imagery.** Make it specific to your story and your protagonist's fears.

Quick ChatGPT Trick

If you're stuck writing a nightmare scene, try:

"Write a short, disturbing nightmare for a horror protagonist who's afraid of losing control."

You'll get something you can drop right into your draft and tweak to fit.

Why Nightmares Work So Well in Horror

Because they're personal, primal, and chaotic. Readers might not be scared of the monster or the haunted house—but everyone knows what it's like to wake up sweating from a nightmare.

When you tap into that universal experience and tie it to your protagonist's struggle, you pull the reader deeper into the horror. You make them question what's real. And you make them feel unsafe—because the horror isn't just outside. It's inside their own mind.

Final Thought

Dreams and nightmares aren't just atmospheric fluff. They're windows into the character's psyche, foreshadowing devices, and tension-building machines. When used well, they become one of the sharpest weapons in your horror storytelling toolkit.

Keeping Creative Control with ChatGPT

By now, you've learned how to plot, structure, and inject horror into every scene of your story. You've also seen how ChatGPT can help you brainstorm ideas, punch up dialogue, build tension, and throw in terrifying twists. But there's one thing you need to remember—no matter how much you rely on AI help: **You are the writer.** ChatGPT is a tool. It can spark ideas, speed up your process, and fill in the gaps—but the story is still yours.

In this chapter, we're going to talk about how to keep creative control while using ChatGPT to write your horror story in one day. Because the last thing you want is a generic, AI-sounding story that reads like every other horror story out there. You want something that feels like it came from your mind—even if you used AI to get it on the page fast.

Why Creative Control Matters

Horror works best when it's **personal.** When it taps into your specific fears, your imagination, your voice. If you lean too hard on AI to do the work without guiding it, your story will feel flat, formulaic, and lifeless.

ChatGPT can generate words. But **you** are the one who knows:

- What scares you
- How you want your characters to feel
- What kind of ending will hit the hardest
- How the tension should rise and fall

Creative control is the difference between a story that **sounds like a horror story** and a story that **feels like a nightmare.**

How to Stay in Control While Using ChatGPT

Here's how you can work with AI without losing your voice or vision:

1. Start With a Clear Vision

Before you even open ChatGPT, know what kind of horror story you want to write:

- What's the core fear?
- Who's the protagonist?
- What's the setting?
- How do you want the reader to feel?

The clearer your vision, the better you can guide ChatGPT's output.

You can even write a short mission statement:

"I want to write a psychological horror story about a woman trapped in a haunted hotel, where the horror is tied to her guilt over her past."

Then, every time you use ChatGPT, you can remind yourself of that mission.

2. Use ChatGPT for Building Blocks—Not the Whole House

ChatGPT is great for brainstorming, outlining, writing scenes, or punching up descriptions. But don't just copy-paste and move on. Treat the AI output as raw material—something to refine, rewrite, or reshape into your voice.

You can ask for:

- Story ideas
- Character profiles
- Scary descriptions
- Dialogue drafts
- Scene outlines

Then, go back and rewrite them so they feel like **you.**

3. Direct the AI Like a Writing Assistant

Think of ChatGPT like a writing assistant, not a ghostwriter. You're the boss. Be specific with your prompts. Tell it what you want, how you want it, and what you're going to do with it.

Instead of:

"Write a horror story."

Say:

"Write a tense scene where the protagonist hears something moving under their bed but is too scared to look."

4. Always Add Your Voice

Even if ChatGPT gives you great dialogue or a creepy setting, go back and sprinkle your personality in. Add a turn of phrase only you would use. Cut unnecessary words. Change pacing. Make sure it sounds like something **you** would write.

5. Keep the Emotional Core Yours

Horror isn't just about monsters and gore. It's about fear, loss, guilt, survival. Those emotions should come from you. Don't let ChatGPT decide how your characters feel—**you** decide, and then use the AI to help you express it clearly.

6. Stay in Charge of Plot Choices

When you're outlining with ChatGPT, you'll often get plot suggestions. Some will be good, some will be bland, some will be clichés. You don't have to accept everything the AI gives you.

Use ChatGPT to list options—but **you** choose the path.

Example prompt:

"Give me five different ways this horror scene could end."

Then pick the one that excites you—or combine two and make it better.

7. Edit Like a Maniac

Once you've used ChatGPT to help you write your story draft, take the time to go back through and **edit ruthlessly.**

Cut boring lines. Rewrite clunky sentences. Make the scares sharper. Make the dialogue snappier. Make the protagonist's emotions clearer.

Your editing pass is where you make the story yours.

8. Use ChatGPT as a Safety Net—Not a Crutch

There's nothing wrong with leaning on AI to move fast, especially if you're trying to write a story in one day. But always keep your creative instincts in the driver's seat. The AI can help you climb the mountain—but **you're the one planting the flag at the top.**

Quick ChatGPT Trick

If you ever feel like your story is sounding too bland or generic, you can prompt:

"How can I make this horror scene more unique and in my own voice?"

Why This Works

ChatGPT is an incredible tool—but it's only as good as the writer using it. When you use it intentionally, with a clear vision and creative control, it speeds up your process without flattening your story.

The goal is to end up with a horror story that sounds like you wrote it—not like an AI wrote it. One that terrifies, unsettles, and lingers with the reader because it came from your imagination.

Final Thought

Writing a horror story in one day doesn't mean giving up creative control. It means using every tool at your disposal—including ChatGPT—to write faster, smarter, and scarier. But the story is still yours. The fear, the tension, the characters, the nightmare—they all come from you.

How to Test if Your Horror Story Is Actually Scary

You've done the work. You've created terrifying characters, built creepy settings, plotted nasty twists, and maybe even written your entire horror story in one day with ChatGPT. But here's the question you need to ask yourself before you hit publish, submit, or share:

Is it actually scary?

It's a strange thing about horror writing—what seems terrifying in your head doesn't always hit the reader the same way. What creeps you out may fall flat on the page. So how do you know if your horror story is doing what it's supposed to do?

In this chapter, we're going to talk about how to test if your horror story is genuinely scary, how to fix it if it isn't, and how ChatGPT can help you sharpen the fear factor fast.

Start by Scaring Yourself

This is the first test—and it's the most important.

When you read your own story, does it make you uncomfortable?

Do you feel tension? Dread? A little shiver down your spine?

If you're reading your story back and it feels flat, predictable, or mechanical—it's probably not scary enough.

You can use ChatGPT to help here:

"Read this horror story and tell me what parts are scary and what parts fall flat."

The AI will quickly point out which sections lack tension or atmosphere.

Get Someone Else to Read It

You can't always trust yourself to judge your own work. You're too close to it. So once you've finished your story:

- Send it to a trusted friend who likes horror.
- Ask them to read it in one sitting.
- Tell them you don't want compliments—you want honest feedback.
  Where did they feel tense? Where did they lose interest? What stuck with them afterward?

If they say things like:

"That part really creeped me out,"

"I wasn't expecting that twist,"

"I kept looking over my shoulder while reading,"

you're on the right track.

If they say:

"It was fine, but I've seen that before,"

"I didn't really feel scared,"

you need to go back and sharpen your story.

Look for Emotional Reactions

You want your reader to feel something physical while reading. Goosebumps. A tight chest. That little knot in their stomach.

You can even ask test readers:

"What physical reaction did you have while reading?"

If they say **none,** that's a red flag.

Use ChatGPT as a Fear Detector

ChatGPT can't feel fear—but it can analyze your story for tension, pacing, and emotional beats. Try:

"Analyze this horror story and tell me if the tension builds effectively."

Or:

"Point out the scariest scene in this story and explain why it works."

You can also use it to run specific tests:

"Does this scene create a sense of dread or tension?"

Check for Predictability

One reason horror stories fail is because the reader sees everything coming. Go back through your story and ask:

- Did I use clichés?
- Are the scares too obvious?
- Are the twists too easy to guess?

You can ask ChatGPT:

"Tell me if this horror story is predictable and suggest ways to make it less so."

Watch for Pacing Problems

A common reason horror stories lose their scare factor is poor pacing. If your story drags, readers stop feeling tense. If you jump from scare to scare without any buildup, the tension feels cheap.

Ask yourself:

- Are there quiet moments where tension can build?
- Are the scary scenes spaced out to let readers breathe—and then hit harder?
- Does the story build toward a climax?

You can get ChatGPT to help analyze this too: **"Analyze the pacing of this horror story and tell me where it loses tension."**

Test the Ending

Your ending is crucial. Horror readers want one of two things:

- A devastating, terrifying, lingering ending.
- Or a cathartic, hard-earned survival.

If your ending is too neat, too happy, or too confusing, the entire story can fall flat.

Ask yourself:

- Does the ending pay off the tension I built?
- Will readers remember it tomorrow?
- Does it stick the knife in—or twist it?

You can use ChatGPT to help sharpen the ending: **"Suggest three ways to make this horror story ending more terrifying."**

The Gut Test

Finally, read your story out loud—alone, in a quiet room, preferably at night.

If you start to feel a little uncomfortable while reading—good. That means the horror is working.

If you get to the end and feel nothing—you need to go back and figure out why.

What If It's Not Scary Enough?

If you test your story and realize it's missing the fear factor, here's what you can do:

- **Add more sensory detail.** Use sound, smell, and texture to make scenes visceral.
- **Raise the stakes.** Make the protagonist's danger clearer and more immediate.
- **Slow down key scenes.** Let tension build before the horror hits.
- **Sharpen the protagonist's fear.** Readers feel what the characters feel.
- **Cut predictable beats.** Replace them with fresh, unsettling twists.
- **Make the ending hit harder.** Leave something unanswered, dark, or disturbing.

You can use ChatGPT to help you fix weak spots fast: **"Suggest ways to make this horror scene more intense and scary."**

Final Thought

Writing horror isn't about how many monsters you can throw at the reader. It's about how you make them **feel.** If you can make them uncomfortable, anxious, breathless, or haunted—you've done your job.

Use the tools in this chapter to test your story before you hit publish. Make sure it's not just a collection of creepy words—but an experience that crawls under the reader's skin and stays there.

Editing and Refining Your Horror Story in One Day

So you've done it—you've written your horror story in one day. You've poured fear onto the page, used ChatGPT to help with characters, plot, dialogue, and pacing, and now you're staring at your rough draft. But here's the next crucial step, the step that separates an okay horror story from one that's truly terrifying: **editing and refining.**

And yes, you can absolutely do this part in the same day too. It just requires a focused, ruthless mindset and a clear plan.

In this chapter, I'm going to show you how to clean up, sharpen, and tighten your horror story fast without sacrificing quality, so when you're done, you'll have a story that drips with dread, tension, and terrifying clarity.

First, Take a Short Break

After you finish your draft, step away from it. Even for just an hour. Let your brain cool down. You've been in writing mode—now you need to switch to **editor mode.**

Go for a walk. Make a coffee. Let the story settle so you can come back to it with fresh eyes.

Step One: Read It Like a Reader

When you sit back down, read the story start to finish without editing. Pretend you've never seen it before. Pay attention to your gut reactions:

- Where does the tension drop?
- Which scenes drag?
- Which lines make you feel something?
- Where did you get bored or confused?

If you feel your pulse quicken or your stomach tighten—**good.** That's where the horror is working.

If you feel like skimming or lose interest—that's where you need to edit.

Step Two: Trim the Fat

Horror stories work best when they're lean and mean. If there are paragraphs of over-explanation, unnecessary description, or characters talking too much—**cut them.**

Look for:

- Long sections of backstory
- Repetitive dialogue
- Description that kills tension
- Over-explained internal thoughts

Keep the story moving. Let the tension breathe, but don't let it die.

You can even ask ChatGPT:

"Which parts of this horror story slow down the tension?"

It'll highlight areas you can tighten.

Step Three: Sharpen Your Scares

Go back through your key horror scenes and make sure they're as effective as possible.

Ask yourself:

- Is the setting clear and creepy?
- Are the sensory details vivid?
- Is the protagonist's fear palpable?
- Is there tension before the scare—and a consequence after?

If a scare falls flat, rewrite it. Make the moment more visual, visceral, or surprising.

You can also ask ChatGPT to help rewrite scenes:

"Rewrite this scene to make it scarier and more intense."

Step Four: Punch Up Dialogue

Horror dialogue should be tight, tense, and emotional. No long monologues or casual chit-chat.

As you read, cut unnecessary words. Make sentences short, sharp, and terrified.

If a character's speech feels too polished, rewrite it so it sounds panicked, desperate, or broken.

You can ask ChatGPT:

"Rewrite this horror dialogue to sound more terrified and natural."

Step Five: Clarify the Plot

When you're writing fast, it's easy to leave loose threads or confusing plot points. On your editing pass:

- Make sure the protagonist's goal is clear.
- Make sure the stakes rise throughout the story.
- Make sure the climax hits hard.
- Make sure the ending feels earned and impactful.

You can even ask ChatGPT to double-check:

"Are there any plot holes or unresolved questions in this horror story?"

Step Six: Check Pacing

Read the story again, this time focusing on pacing. Your horror story should build tension, release it briefly, and then crank it higher.

Look for:

- Scenes that drag without adding tension
- Too many scares without buildup
- Long sections of exposition between horror beats

If you find a slow section, ask yourself:

- Can I cut this?
- Can I make it creepier?
- Can I move the horror closer?

Step Seven: Strengthen the Ending

The last thing you want is a weak ending. Your story should leave the reader breathless, horrified, or haunted.

Re-read your final scene and ask:

- Does it pay off the tension?
- Does it stick with the reader?
- Does it leave a lingering sense of dread or relief?

If not, rewrite it.

You can also ask ChatGPT:

"Suggest three ways to make the ending of this horror story more terrifying."

Step Eight: Polish the Language

Once you've fixed structure, scares, and pacing, do a quick language pass:

- Cut filler words
- Tighten sentences
- Make descriptions sharper
- Watch out for overused words

You want your prose to feel sharp and clean so the horror shines through.

Step Nine: Final Read-Aloud Pass

When you think you're done—**read the story out loud.**

You'll catch awkward sentences, clunky dialogue, and flat descriptions instantly.

If you trip over a line or get bored while reading, revise.

Quick ChatGPT Trick

If you want to do a fast polish, you can paste your story and prompt:

"Edit this horror story to improve flow and tension without changing the plot."

Why This Works

Editing isn't about fixing mistakes—it's about making your horror story hit harder. Every edit should sharpen the scares, tighten the pacing, and make the reader more uncomfortable.

And yes—you can absolutely do all this in one day.

Write fast. Edit smart. Get the story scary and clean without overthinking.

Final Thought

The first draft is you telling yourself the story. The edit is you telling it to your reader. And in horror, that difference is everything.

In the next chapter, we're going to show you how to package and format your freshly edited horror story, so it's ready to share, publish, or scare the hell out of someone.

Because now that your story is terrifying—you need to deliver it properly.

Packaging and Formatting Your Story for Publishing

You've done the heavy lifting. You've brainstormed, plotted, written, and edited your horror story—all in one day. It's terrifying, tight, and dripping with dread. But you're not done yet. There's one more step before you can send your story out into the world: **packaging and formatting.**

This step is often overlooked by new writers, but it's critical. If your story isn't clean, professional, and properly formatted, it doesn't matter how scary it is—readers, agents, publishers, and editors will judge it before they've even read the first word.

In this chapter, we're going to walk you through how to format, package, and prepare your horror story for publishing or sharing. And yes—you can get this done quickly, right after you've finished editing.

Why Formatting and Presentation Matter

Horror is all about tension, atmosphere, and pacing. But none of that will matter if your story looks messy or unprofessional. Poor formatting pulls readers out of the story. It sends a signal that you didn't care enough to present your story properly.

The goal of formatting is simple:

Make your story easy to read.

That's it. Clean, clear, and distraction-free.

Basic Formatting for Short Horror Stories

If you're submitting your story to a magazine, anthology, contest, or agent, here's the standard format most people expect:

- **Font:** Times New Roman or Courier, 12-point
- **Spacing:** Double-spaced
- **Margins:** 1-inch margins on all sides
- **Alignment:** Left-aligned (no justified text)
- **Paragraphs:** Indent the first line of each paragraph; no extra spacing between paragraphs
- **Title and Name:** At the top left of the first page, include your name, email, and word count
- **Page Numbers:** Include your last name and page number in the header of each page
- **File Format:** Usually .doc, .docx, or .rtf (always check the publisher's guidelines)

If you're self-publishing or sharing the story online, you can be more flexible, but the same rule applies: **make it clean and readable.**

Title and Cover Page

Even if you're not sending your story to a publisher, make it look like something special. Add a simple cover page with:

- Story title
- Your name
- Date
- Optional: A short tagline or teaser sentence

You can also use ChatGPT to help you brainstorm a creepy, punchy title: **"Suggest ten creepy titles for a horror story about a haunted forest."**

Writing a Brief Synopsis (Optional but Helpful)

If you're submitting your story anywhere, you may need a short synopsis. One or two paragraphs summarizing the plot without giving away every twist.

You can use ChatGPT to help you draft this quickly: **"Write a two-paragraph synopsis of this horror story."**

Creating an Author Bio (Optional)

If you're publishing online, submitting to magazines, or packaging your story as an ebook, you'll want a short author bio. Keep it brief and interesting.

Example: *"author name" is a horror writer who believes the scariest monsters live inside our own minds. When he's not writing, he's hunting for the perfect haunted location.*

ChatGPT can help you write a bio too: **"Write a 50-word author bio for a horror writer."**

EBook and Self-Publishing Formats

If you're planning to self-publish your story, you'll want to format it as an ebook. Luckily, there are free tools to help:

- **Reedsy Book Editor** (clean, simple, and free)
- **Calibre** (for converting to .epub or .mobi formats)
- **Vellum** (for professional-looking ebooks, Mac only)

Use clear chapter headings, clean page breaks, and a simple font. Horror is about mood—don't clutter your ebook with fancy fonts or distracting graphics.

Adding a Cover (Optional but Encouraged)

If you're publishing online or as an ebook, you'll want a cover. It doesn't need to be fancy—a simple, atmospheric image works.

You can use AI tools like DALL·E, Midjourney, or Canva to create a creepy, eye-catching cover fast.

If you want, you can even ask ChatGPT: **"Suggest five cover concepts for a horror short story about a cursed mirror."**

Publishing Options

Once your story is formatted and packaged, you have options:

- **Submit to horror magazines or anthologies** (check submission guidelines)
- **Publish on your website or blog**
- **Share it on platforms like Wattpad, Medium, or Reddit's r/nosleep**
- **Self-publish on Amazon Kindle, Draft2Digital, Kobo, or Smashwords**
- **Package it as part of a horror short story collection**

Each option has different pros and cons. If you're just starting out, sharing your story online is a great way to build an audience fast.

Quick ChatGPT Trick

If you're unsure where to publish, ask: **"List ten websites or platforms where I can publish a horror short story."**

Final Read-Through

Before you hit submit, publish, or share—read your story one more time. Make sure there are no typos, formatting glitches, or sloppy sentences. Clean presentation matters.

Final Thought

Your horror story deserves to be read. You've done the hard work—now package it so people can experience it the way you intended. Make it clean, creepy, and professional.

Examples of Good Prompts for Story Design and Structure

You've made it to the end. You've learned how to generate scary ideas, build terrifying characters, crank up tension, and even package your horror story professionally—all in one productive, terrifying day. But before we close this book, I want to leave you with one of the most powerful tools in your writing arsenal: **well-crafted prompts.**

Your secret weapon for writing a horror story quickly, creatively, and effectively is knowing how to talk to ChatGPT. The better your prompts, the better the results. So in this chapter, I'm going to give you a list of example prompts you can use when designing and structuring your horror story. These aren't generic—these are specific, actionable prompts that will save you time, keep you focused, and help you shape your story into something readers won't forget.

Why Prompts Matter

A lot of writers treat ChatGPT like a magic box: "Write me a horror story."

That's fine—but you'll get average, mechanical results.

If you want something fresh, personal, and terrifying, you need to give the AI clear, specific instructions.

Think of ChatGPT like a writing assistant. It can help you outline, brainstorm, structure, and even write scenes—but only if you give it **good direction.**

Prompts for Idea Generation

When you're just starting and need a fast, scary idea:

- **"Give me five original horror story concepts based on fear of the unknown."**
- **"Create three horror story premises set in an abandoned amusement park."**
- **"Brainstorm five unique horror villains that haven't been done before."**
- **"Give me three horror story ideas that combine supernatural horror and psychological horror."**

Prompts for Structure and Plot

When you're ready to outline and structure your story:

- **"Outline a three-act structure for a horror story about a haunted mirror."**
- **"Break down the main story beats for a survival horror story in a forest."**
- **"Give me a story structure for a horror story where the protagonist slowly realizes they're the villain."**
- **"Write a detailed outline for a horror story that builds to a shocking twist ending."**
- **"What are five key plot points I should include in a psychological horror story?"**

Prompts for Character Design

When you need help fleshing out your protagonist, antagonist, or side characters:

- **"Create a character profile for a horror protagonist who is terrified of losing control."**
- **"Describe a horror villain who is charming but deadly."**
- **"Give me five creepy supporting characters for a small-town horror story."**

- **"Outline the character arc of a protagonist in a horror story who survives but is broken by the experience."**

Prompts for Setting and Atmosphere

To make your world terrifying and immersive:

- **"Describe a haunted asylum in vivid sensory detail."**
- **"List five unsettling locations for a modern horror story."**
- **"Create a creepy small-town setting with dark secrets for a horror story."**
- **"Write an atmospheric description of a forest at night during a horror scene."**

Prompts for Pacing and Tension

When you want to make sure your story builds tension effectively:

- **"How can I structure my horror story so that the tension steadily rises to a climax?"**
- **"List five ways to slow down a horror story scene to build suspense."**
- **"Suggest how to pace the middle section of a horror story so readers stay scared."**

Prompts for Dialogue and Character Interaction

To keep your dialogue creepy, realistic, and tension-filled:

- **"Write a tense dialogue exchange between two characters hiding from a killer."**
- **"Give me five creepy things a horror villain might say to the protagonist."**
- **"Rewrite this horror dialogue so it sounds more natural and terrified."**

Prompts for Twists and Turns

When you want to keep readers guessing:

- **"List five unexpected twists I could use in a horror story."**
- **"Give me three ways to mislead the reader in a horror story without cheating."**
- **"Suggest a shocking final twist for a horror story where the protagonist thinks they've escaped."**

Prompts for Themes and Subtext

When you want your horror story to have something deeper:

- **"What themes can I explore in a horror story about isolation?"**
- **"How can I weave the theme of guilt into a psychological horror story?"**
- **"List five symbolic images I can use in a horror story about grief."**

Prompts for Editing and Refining

Once your first draft is done and you want to clean it up:

- **"Analyze this horror story and tell me which parts are scary and which fall flat."**
- **"Suggest ways to make this horror story more tense and frightening."**
- **"Rewrite this horror scene to increase tension and fear."**
- **"Check this story for clichés and suggest fresh alternatives."**

Quick ChatGPT Trick

When in doubt, you can always use this catch-all prompt: **"Help me design and structure a horror story about [insert your idea]. Include plot points, characters, setting, and a scary ending."**

How to Keep Control of Your Story

Remember, the goal isn't to let ChatGPT write the entire story for you—it's to speed up the process and fill in the blanks. You still need to bring the emotion, tension, and voice. These prompts are here to help you:

- Save time
- Stay focused
- Stay inspired
- Keep the horror flowing

Final Thought

Writing a horror story in one day isn't about rushing—it's about writing smart. These prompts will help you do exactly that. You can use them to plan your next horror story, refine one you've already written, or even challenge yourself to write a brand-new nightmare in a single afternoon.

Because now that you know how to generate, structure, write, and package a horror story fast—nothing's stopping you from creating horror over and over again.

The monsters are waiting. And now, you're ready to unleash them.

Examples of Good Prompts for Designing Compelling Characters

You can have the scariest plot in the world, the creepiest haunted house, and the nastiest twist ending—but if your characters are flat, your horror story will fall apart. What makes horror stick isn't just the monster; it's the **people** being hunted, haunted, or broken.

A great horror story needs characters readers care about, root for, or fear. But when you're writing fast—especially when you're knocking out a story in one day—you might not have time to spend hours building deep character profiles from scratch.

That's where **good ChatGPT prompts** come in. In this chapter, I'll give you specific, actionable prompts you can use to quickly design compelling, believable, and memorable horror characters.

Because if your readers don't care about who's in danger, they won't care about the danger at all.

Prompts for Creating Protagonists

Your protagonist is the anchor of your horror story. They don't need to be perfect—in fact, they're better when they're flawed. Here's how to use ChatGPT to help you design them fast:

- **"Create a horror protagonist who is brave but emotionally broken."**
- **"Give me a character profile for a horror story protagonist who has a dark secret."**
- **"Describe a protagonist for a psychological horror story who is unreliable and mentally unstable."**
- **"Write a brief backstory for a horror protagonist who is trying to escape their past."**
- **"List five personal fears that would make a horror protagonist vulnerable."**

You can also use multi-step prompts: **"Give me a horror protagonist's name, age, occupation, flaw, secret, and fear."**

Then build from there.

Prompts for Designing Villains and Antagonists

Your villain doesn't have to be a monster. It can be a ghost, a curse, a serial killer, or even the protagonist themselves. Either way, they need to be compelling.

Try:

- **"Create a horror villain who is charming on the outside but monstrous underneath."**
- **"Describe a supernatural antagonist who feeds on fear."**
- **"List five traits that make a horror story villain truly terrifying."**
- **"Write a character profile for a horror villain who manipulates people rather than killing them."**
- **"Give me three ideas for horror villains who don't physically appear but control the story."**

If you want your villain to have depth, ask: **"What is the tragic backstory of this horror villain?"**

or

"List five motivations that could drive a horror antagonist."

Prompts for Supporting Characters

Side characters matter in horror. They can raise the stakes, add tension, or die horribly to show how serious the threat is.

Prompts:

- **"Give me five creepy supporting characters for a haunted house horror story."**
- **"Create a best friend character who will betray the protagonist in a horror story."**
- **"List three types of horror supporting characters who make the situation worse."**
- **"Describe a horror story side character who knows more than they're telling."**

You can also ask ChatGPT to give you character quirks: **"List five strange or unsettling personality traits for a horror story character."**

Prompts for Character Relationships

Horror hits harder when the characters' relationships are tense, broken, or complicated.

Prompts:

- **"Describe the relationship between a horror protagonist and their estranged sibling."**
- **"Create a love triangle dynamic in a horror story where one person is hiding something sinister."**
- **"List three ways a protagonist's relationship with their parent could be used in a horror story."**

You can even ask: **"Write a tense conversation between two horror characters who don't trust each other."**

Prompts for Character Arcs

Good horror characters change. Whether they survive, die, or lose their minds, they should transform during the story.

Prompts:

- **"Describe the character arc of a horror protagonist who starts out confident but ends broken."**
- **"Outline the arc of a horror villain who slowly reveals their true nature."**
- **"Give me three possible endings for a protagonist's journey in a survival horror story."**
- **"List five ways a horror story can change a character forever."**

Prompts for Character-Driven Horror

If you want to build your entire story around your characters (which you should), try these:

- **"Design a horror story concept based entirely on a protagonist's worst fear."**
- **"Give me a horror story idea where the antagonist is a reflection of the protagonist's flaw."**
- **"Outline a horror plot where every supporting character is a manifestation of the protagonist's guilt."**

Prompts to Add Depth and Complexity

Your characters shouldn't just be victims or villains. Give them layers, secrets, and contradictions.

Prompts:

- **"List five personality traits that would make a horror protagonist sympathetic but flawed."**
- **"Give me a dark secret for a horror story character that will be revealed at the climax."**
- **"Write a character profile for a horror protagonist who fears becoming the monster."**
- **"Describe a horror character whose deepest fear is hurting the people they love."**

Quick ChatGPT Trick

If you want to build characters fast, try:

"Create three detailed character profiles (protagonist, antagonist, supporting character) for a horror story set in an abandoned asylum."

You'll get names, traits, backstories, flaws, and fears—all in one prompt.

Final Thought

Horror works because we care about who's in danger. We fear for them, or fear what they'll become. Using smart, clear prompts will help you build characters quickly and effectively without losing depth.

These prompts aren't here to replace your creativity—they're here to unlock it, fast.

Examples of Good Prompts for World Building

You can have the creepiest characters, the nastiest monster, and the most shocking twist, but if your horror story doesn't have a world that feels real, atmospheric, and terrifying—your readers won't feel trapped inside the nightmare. That's where **world building** comes in.

And I don't just mean creating fantasy kingdoms or futuristic cities. In horror, world building is about crafting the unsettling setting, the rules of the nightmare, and the creeping sense that something isn't right, whether you're in a haunted house, a small town with dark secrets, or a hospital where no one ever leaves.

The good news? You don't have to spend weeks creating your horror world. With **smart prompts** and ChatGPT's help, you can build an immersive, terrifying world in a matter of minutes—perfect when you're writing your horror story in one day.

In this chapter, I'll give you clear, specific, and effective prompts you can use to quickly build the world of your horror story without slowing down your writing process.

Prompts for Building Horror Settings

You want your setting to feel alive (or undead), oppressive, eerie, or even hostile. Here are some solid prompts to help you design creepy locations:

- **"Describe an abandoned hospital where something sinister happened, using sensory details."**
- **"Give me five unique and creepy small-town settings for a horror story."**
- **"Create a detailed setting for a psychological horror story that feels claustrophobic."**
- **"Describe a forest that feels alive and dangerous in a horror story."**
- **"List five unsettling locations where people mysteriously disappear."**

You can also get atmospheric details: **"Describe the sights, sounds, and smells of a cursed Victorian mansion."**

Prompts for Establishing Rules of the World

Every horror world has its own rules—even if the characters don't know them yet. Use these prompts to quickly establish the logic (or lack thereof) in your horror story:

- **"List the supernatural rules of a horror world where mirrors are portals to another dimension."**
- **"Explain the unspoken town rules in a small-town horror story."**
- **"Describe the curse and its conditions in a horror story set in an ancient village."**
- **"Create the rules of engagement for a horror world where ghosts can only appear at 3 a.m."**

You can also ask: **"What are five unique horror story world rules that make survival almost impossible?"**

Prompts for Local Legends and Lore

Local folklore, urban legends, and whispered stories add depth and creepiness to your horror world.

Prompts:

- **"Invent a creepy urban legend told in a remote mountain town."**
- **"Describe the ghost story that parents tell their children in this horror village."**
- **"List five disturbing myths about an abandoned asylum."**
- **"Create a folk tale tied to the curse in a horror story."**

Prompts for World History and Backstory

The horror in your story didn't start when your protagonist arrived. Use these prompts to quickly fill in the world's dark history:

- **"Summarize the tragic history of a haunted hotel in a horror story."**
- **"Describe a past event that left a supernatural scar on this horror town."**
- **"List five historical events that could explain why this horror world is cursed."**
- **"Write a brief news article about the strange disappearances in this horror setting."**

Prompts for Creating Atmosphere and Mood

The vibe of your world is everything in horror. You want the reader to feel dread from the first sentence.

Prompts:

- **"Describe the oppressive atmosphere of a foggy, empty city at midnight."**
- **"List five details that make a small-town horror setting feel sinister."**
- **"Write a paragraph describing how the protagonist feels walking into this abandoned house."**
- **"What sensory details can I use to make a horror story setting feel claustrophobic and unsafe?"**

Prompts for Building Unseen Horrors

One of the best things about horror world building is what you **don't** show. Use these prompts to make your world feel dangerous even when nothing's happening:

- **"List five subtle signs that something is wrong in a horror town."**
- **"Describe how nature itself feels threatening in this horror world."**
- **"Give me eerie background details that suggest an unseen presence."**
- **"What creepy objects can I scatter through a horror story setting to build dread?"**

Prompts for World-Building Specific to Subgenres

You can also tailor your prompts to the type of horror you're writing:

Supernatural Horror:

- **"Create a gothic horror world where ghosts are part of everyday life."**

Psychological Horror:

- **"Describe a horror setting that reflects the protagonist's crumbling sanity."**

Slasher Horror:

- **"List five isolated locations perfect for a slasher horror story."**

Survival Horror:

- **"Design a post-apocalyptic world overrun by supernatural creatures."**

Quick ChatGPT Trick

If you're building your story fast and need a fully fleshed-out world in minutes, use this mega-prompt:

"Create a detailed horror story world including setting, local legends, history, atmosphere, and the rules of the horror."

You'll get a detailed framework that you can customize and plug straight into your draft.

Final Thought

World building isn't just for epic fantasy writers. In horror, your world is the thing that traps your characters, suffocates them, and keeps readers turning the page long after the last scream. With the right prompts, you can build immersive, terrifying horror worlds in minutes without slowing down your writing process.

Now that you know how to design your world fast, creepy, and effectively, you've got every tool you need to write a horror story in a single, productive, blood-curdling day.

Examples of Prompts for Ideas about Horror Stories

You've now got all the tools to write, edit, structure, and package your horror story in one day. But let's face it—sometimes, the hardest part is just coming up with the **idea.** You sit down, you want to write something scary, but your brain is blank. That's where good prompts come in.

A solid idea prompt is like a lit match. It doesn't give you the entire fire, but it gives you enough spark to ignite your imagination and start building a nightmare. And when you're writing fast, you don't want to waste time staring at a blank screen—you want something that will trigger a story instantly.

In this chapter, I'll give you specific, effective prompts you can use to generate fresh, terrifying horror story ideas quickly. You can use these prompts to create an entire plot or just to kickstart your imagination when you're stuck.

Prompts for Concept Ideas

When you need a complete, ready-to-go horror story concept:

- **"Give me five original horror story concepts based on the fear of isolation."**
- **"What's a fresh horror story idea about a haunted piece of technology?"**
- **"Create three horror story concepts that combine supernatural and psychological horror."**
- **"Give me a horror story idea where the protagonist is the monster but doesn't realize it."**
- **"Suggest five short horror story ideas that could happen in a single location."**

Prompts for Setting-Based Ideas

If you want your story to start with the location and build from there:

- **"Give me three horror story ideas set in an abandoned hospital."**
- **"What's a horror story concept that takes place entirely in an elevator?"**
- **"List five eerie, unusual locations that would make great horror story settings."**
- **"Create a horror story plot set in a small town with a deadly secret."**

Prompts for Character-Based Ideas

Sometimes, the best horror stories start with a character:

- **"Give me a horror story idea about a protagonist with a dark secret."**
- **"What's a horror story concept where the villain is a trusted family member?"**
- **"Suggest five horror story ideas where the protagonist's greatest fear comes true."**
- **"Create a horror story idea about a character who can see other people's nightmares."**

Prompts for Theme-Driven Ideas

If you want your horror story to explore something deeper:

- **"List five horror story ideas that explore the theme of guilt."**
- **"What's a horror story concept about the dangers of obsession?"**

- **"Give me a horror story idea where the theme is the cost of survival."**
- **"Suggest five horror story concepts based on the theme of trust and betrayal."**

Prompts for Twist-Based Ideas

If you want your story to revolve around a shocking twist:

- **"Give me a horror story idea with a twist ending where the protagonist is the villain."**
- **"Suggest three horror story concepts where the supernatural threat is a misdirection."**
- **"What's a horror story idea with a double twist ending?"**

Prompts for Subgenre Ideas

Tailor your prompts to specific horror subgenres:

Supernatural Horror:

- **"Give me three ghost story concepts with fresh, original premises."**

Slasher Horror:

- **"Create a slasher horror story idea with an unexpected setting."**

Psychological Horror:

- **"What's a horror story idea that explores the protagonist's crumbling sanity?"**

Survival Horror:

- **"Suggest three survival horror story concepts set in extreme environments."**

Folk Horror:

- **"Create a folk horror story idea based on an ancient ritual."**

Prompts for "What If" Scenarios

One of the fastest ways to generate horror ideas is to play the "What if..." game.

Prompts:

- **"What if everyone in a small town disappeared overnight—but one person remained?"**
- **"What if a person's shadow started moving on its own?"**
- **"What if a haunted house kept changing its layout every night?"**
- **"What if the protagonist's childhood imaginary friend came back—and it wasn't friendly?"**
- **"What if the protagonist woke up every morning missing a memory—and something was hunting them while they slept?"**

Prompts for Combining Horror Elements

You can ask ChatGPT to mash different horror elements together:

- **"Create a horror story idea that combines cosmic horror and body horror."**
- **"Give me three horror story concepts that blend science fiction and supernatural horror."**
- **"Suggest a horror story idea that combines a haunted location, a cursed object, and psychological breakdown."**

Quick ChatGPT Trick

If you're in a hurry and need something specific, try:

"Give me a complete horror story concept including protagonist, antagonist, setting, conflict, and twist ending."

You can also ask for lists: **"List ten fresh horror story ideas I can write in one day."**

How to Use These Prompts Fast

When you're writing in one day, you don't want to get stuck at the idea stage. Use these prompts like this:

1. Pick a theme, setting, or character.
2. Ask ChatGPT for five or ten story concepts.
3. Choose the one that makes your stomach drop.
4. Expand it into an outline using the prompts from earlier chapters.
5. Write.

Final Thought

The scariest stories don't come from sitting around waiting for inspiration—they come from asking the right questions. When you use clear, creative prompts, you can spark horror ideas anytime, anywhere, and start building nightmares fast. You now have an entire arsenal of prompts at your fingertips. So when you're ready to write your next horror story in one day, you'll never be stuck staring at a blank page—you'll have terrifying ideas ready to go.

Your One-Day Horror Writing Game Plan – From Start to Publish

You've made it to the final stretch. You now have everything you need—the knowledge, the prompts, the structure, and the editing techniques—to write a terrifying, professional-quality horror story in one day. But now, let's get practical. You don't want to just write the story. You want to go from **blank page** to **published story** in less than twenty-four hours.

This chapter is your complete, hour-by-hour game plan for writing, editing, formatting, and publishing your horror story—all in one day. Follow this, and by bedtime tonight, you'll have a finished piece of horror fiction that's ready to scare readers.

Step One: Idea Generation (30 Minutes)

Start by warming up your creativity. Don't overthink—just get ideas flowing. Use the idea prompts from Chapter 63 to help.

Ask ChatGPT: **"Give me five fresh horror story concepts that could be written in one day."**

Pick the one that excites you the most. Don't waste time debating. Choose the idea that makes you say, *"Ooh, that's creepy."*

Step Two: Outline Your Story (45 Minutes)

Use the structure prompts we discussed earlier. Outline your three acts quickly:

- Act 1: Introduce the protagonist, the setting, and the creeping dread.
- Act 2: Escalate the horror, raise the stakes, throw in twists.
- Act 3: Deliver the climax and a powerful ending.

Ask ChatGPT to help: **"Outline a three-act structure for this horror story concept."**

Tweak it to fit your voice and vision. This is your road map—you want to spend more time writing than figuring out what happens next.

Step Three: Flesh Out Your Characters (30 Minutes)

Quickly develop your protagonist, antagonist, and one or two supporting characters. Use the prompts from Chapter 61.

Ask ChatGPT: **"Create character profiles for the protagonist, antagonist, and supporting characters in this horror story."**

You want to know:

- What they want
- What they fear
- How they will change (or not) by the end

Step Four: World Building and Atmosphere (30 Minutes)

Spend a little time making sure your setting is creepy, immersive, and vivid. Use the world-building prompts from Chapter 62.

Prompt example: **"Describe the haunted setting for this horror story using sensory detail."**

You don't need to overdo it. Just enough to give the reader a clear, eerie world to fall into.

Step Five: Write the First Draft (3 to 4 Hours)

Now, dive in. Write your entire first draft in one focused writing session. Follow your outline, use your character profiles, and keep your pacing sharp.

When you get stuck:

- Use ChatGPT to generate dialogue, scene descriptions, or scary details.
- Don't stop to edit. Keep moving.

Your goal is **1,500 to 5,000 words** depending on your target (short story or longer piece).

Step Six: Quick Break (15-30 Minutes)

Walk away. Eat something. Rest your eyes. You've earned it.

Step Seven: First Editing Pass (1 Hour)

Go back through your draft. Read it like a reader.

Look for:

- Plot holes
- Clunky dialogue
- Slow pacing
- Missed opportunities for tension or scares

Use ChatGPT to help: **"Read this horror story and point out where the tension drops."**

Clean up anything obvious.

Step Eight: Second Editing Pass – Polish (30 Minutes)

Now tighten your prose. Cut filler words. Sharpen sentences. Make descriptions more vivid.

Ask ChatGPT: **"Rewrite this horror scene to make it scarier."**

or

"Edit this dialogue to sound more natural and terrified."

Step Nine: Final Read-Through (30 Minutes)

Read the story out loud.

You're listening for:

- Awkward sentences
- Repetitive words
- Moments where the tension dips

Fix anything that feels off.

Step Ten: Formatting and Packaging (30 Minutes)

Follow the guidelines from Chapter 59:

- Proper formatting
- Clean, readable font and spacing
- Title page with your name and story title

Optional:

- Create a quick, simple cover using Canva or an AI image generator
- Write a short author bio and story synopsis

Step Eleven: Publish or Share (15 Minutes)

You've done the work. Now send it out into the world:

- Submit to a horror magazine or contest
- Post it on your blog or website
- Share it on Medium, Reddit's r/nosleep, or Wattpad
- Self-publish as an ebook

You can even compile your one-day horror stories into a collection over time.

Optional: Ask ChatGPT for Suggestions

If you're unsure where to publish: **"List ten platforms where I can publish a short horror story."**

Why This Game Plan Works

This isn't about rushing. It's about **writing smart, fast, and focused.**

By using clear, specific prompts and working in timed blocks, you can write a solid, terrifying horror story without burning yourself out.

You don't have to wait for inspiration. You don't need weeks of planning. You don't need to be a "pro."

You just need a process—and now, you've got one.

Final Thought

You've reached the end of this book. You now know how to:

- Generate terrifying ideas
- Outline quickly
- Build compelling characters
- Create creepy worlds
- Write fast and fearlessly
- Edit and refine your story
- Package and publish it—all in one day

The only thing left to do now... is **start.**

Because horror doesn't wait. And neither should you.

Writing More Horror Stories Fast with ChatGPT

By now, you've learned how to write one terrifying, well-structured, professional-quality horror story in a single day. But here's the real magic of what you've built for yourself: **you can do it again. And again. And again.** This process isn't just a one-time trick. It's a repeatable system you can use to crank out gripping horror stories anytime you want, without sacrificing creativity or quality.

In this chapter, I'm going to show you how to keep the momentum going, how to use ChatGPT to stay fresh and inspired, and how to write multiple horror stories fast, whether you want to build a full collection, publish regularly online, or simply keep sharpening your horror writing skills.

Why Write More Horror Stories?

The more you write, the better you get.

Writing horror stories fast doesn't mean writing junk. It means using your time smartly and tapping into the storytelling machine you've now built.

When you write more stories:

- You develop your voice and style
- You build a portfolio of terrifying tales
- You can publish a short story collection
- You improve your plotting, pacing, and character skills
- You experiment with different subgenres and tones
- You stay creatively sharp

And with ChatGPT as your assistant, you can do this without burning out.

The Simple System: Rinse and Repeat

Here's how to keep writing horror stories quickly:

1. Start with a Fresh Prompt

You've already collected a ton of great prompts in previous chapters. Use them to spark new ideas.

Ask ChatGPT: **"Give me five unique horror story ideas that could be written in one day."**

Pick one. Don't overthink it.

2. Outline Quickly

Use the same structure we've covered:

- Act 1: Introduce the protagonist, the fear, and the world.
- Act 2: Build tension and conflict.
- Act 3: Deliver a terrifying climax and a lingering ending.

Use this quick prompt: **"Outline a three-act structure for a horror story about [insert idea]."**

3. Develop New Characters

Ask ChatGPT to help you build characters fast: **"Create character profiles for the protagonist, antagonist, and two side characters in this horror story."**

Change names, add quirks, adjust flaws, and make them yours.

4. Build a New Setting

Don't reuse the same haunted house every time.

Ask: **"Describe a creepy horror setting I haven't used before."**

Or challenge yourself: **"What's the scariest place I could set a horror story that isn't a house or a forest?"**

5. Write Without Hesitation

Block out three to four hours. Write your draft in one sitting.

If you hit a wall: **"Write a creepy scene where the protagonist hears something moving in the dark."**

or

"Write a tense dialogue exchange between the protagonist and the villain."

Keep going. Get to the end.

6. Edit Smart, Not Slow

Use the same two-pass edit system: First pass—fix plot holes, pacing, character consistency.

Second pass—sharpen dialogue, tighten prose, cut filler.

Use ChatGPT as your editor: **"Point out any weak spots in this horror story." "Rewrite this ending to make it more terrifying."**

7. Format and Package

Follow the packaging process from Chapter 59:

- Clean, readable format
- Simple title page
- Optional cover and author bio

8. Publish or Compile

You can publish your new story immediately or start collecting them for a future anthology.

Imagine writing **ten** horror stories in ten days. By the end of two weeks, you'd have enough for a full book.

Keep Your Creativity Fresh

The trick to writing horror stories fast without burning out is to switch things up:

- Change subgenres: supernatural, psychological, slasher, survival, folk horror.
- Write different types of protagonists: brave, broken, unreliable, selfish.
- Change locations: urban, rural, futuristic, isolated.
- Play with themes: fear of death, fear of the unknown, guilt, grief, obsession.

Every time you sit down, challenge yourself to write a different kind of nightmare.

How ChatGPT Makes It Sustainable

Writing quickly doesn't mean writing poorly—it means writing smart.

ChatGPT can help you:

- Brainstorm fresh ideas fast
- Outline clean story structures
- Create unique, creepy characters
- Punch up your prose
- Polish your dialogue
- Catch pacing problems
- Package your stories professionally

You're still the creator—you're steering the ship—but ChatGPT helps you navigate faster without crashing into creative fatigue.

Build a Horror Habit

If you really want to level up, make horror writing a habit:

- Write one story every weekend.
- Challenge yourself to write three stories in three days.
- Write a 30-day horror challenge—one story per day.

You'll be amazed how quickly your skills sharpen, your voice strengthens, and your portfolio grows.

Final Thought

You started this book wanting to write one horror story in one day. Now, you can do that anytime you want—and you can do it again and again. You've built a system that works. You've learned how to take an idea, flesh it out, structure it, write it, edit it, and publish it—all in a single day. And with every story you write, you'll get better. Your worlds will get scarier. Your characters will become more complex. Your readers will keep coming back for the next nightmare. Because now, you don't just know how to write a horror story—you know how to keep writing them, fast and fearlessly.

I hope you found inspiration within these pages. If you liked this book, please leave a review where you bought it. Thank you from the author.

Don't miss out!

Visit the website below and you can sign up to receive emails whenever Andrew Parry publishes a new book. There's no charge and no obligation.

https://books2read.com/r/B-A-FROLC-CSHFG

BOOKS 2 READ

Connecting independent readers to independent writers.

www.ingramcontent.com/pod-product-compliance
Lightning Source LLC
LaVergne TN
LVHW082337200926
848481LV00012B/3367
9798230356011